TABLE OF CONTENTS

FOREWARD

We have a wonderful God who loves us more than we can ever imagine. His mercies are new every morning. If you are a Christian, you have nothing to fear because God is watching over you. God has reminded us that He does not give His loved ones a "spirit of fear, but of power, love and sound mind" 2 Timothy 1:7.

But we live in fearful days. We have a worldwide pandemic running wild across our land. We have unrest in our cities. Instead of unity, there is a division fueled by hate in our people. With destructive storms battering our crops and hurricanes destroying our coasts, our weather seems to be increasingly vicious. We have uncontrolled fires in several states and earthquakes at levels we have never seen. There are wars being fought across our world. Because of all these disasters, the economies of the world are teetering.

We have had all these events occur in our history, but perhaps not at the level of intensity that we see today. It just feels different. In Matthew 24, Jesus said that all these things must take place before the end will come. They are signs that He will soon return for us, His Church.

We can know the events the prophets foretold, but we just do not know exactly when they will take place. From Genesis to Revelation, Godly prophets have written about the future. Many of these prophecies have been fulfilled already but others have not yet been realized. Every prophecy in the Bible has been fulfilled as it was written, or it will be.

The purpose of this study is to review these prophecies to show the faithfulness of our God to do what He says He will do. When fulfilled prophecies are seen to be valid, it strengthens our faith that the rest of God's promises will also be fulfilled. If we know Him we have no reason to fear. God has always taken care of His people and He always will. My prayer is that this study will give you the strength to confidently face each day, knowing that God is in control and has a glorious future for you.

John Pruitt
December 2020

TIMELINE: CREATION TO CHRIST

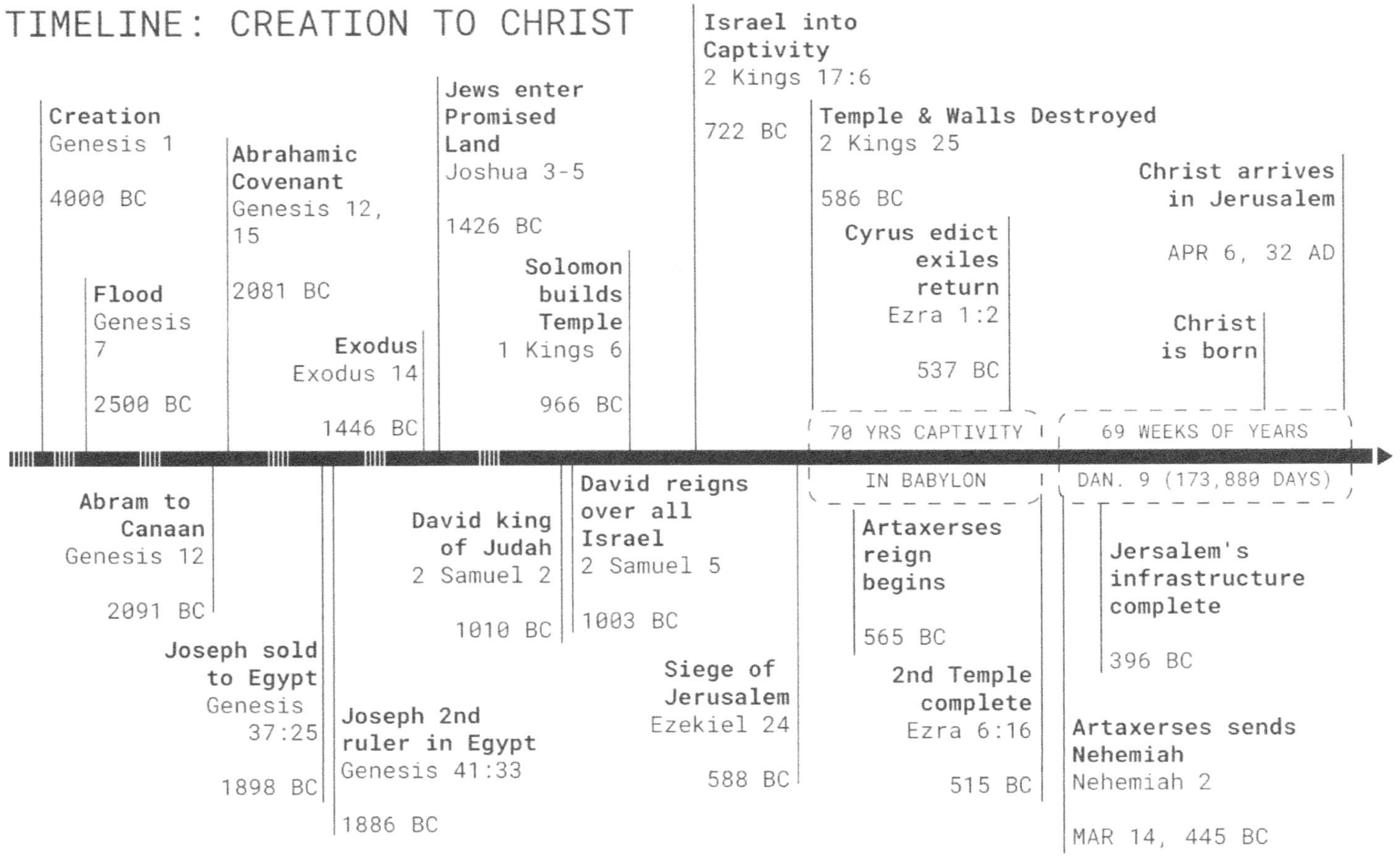

TIMELINE: CHRIST TO ETERNITY FUTURE

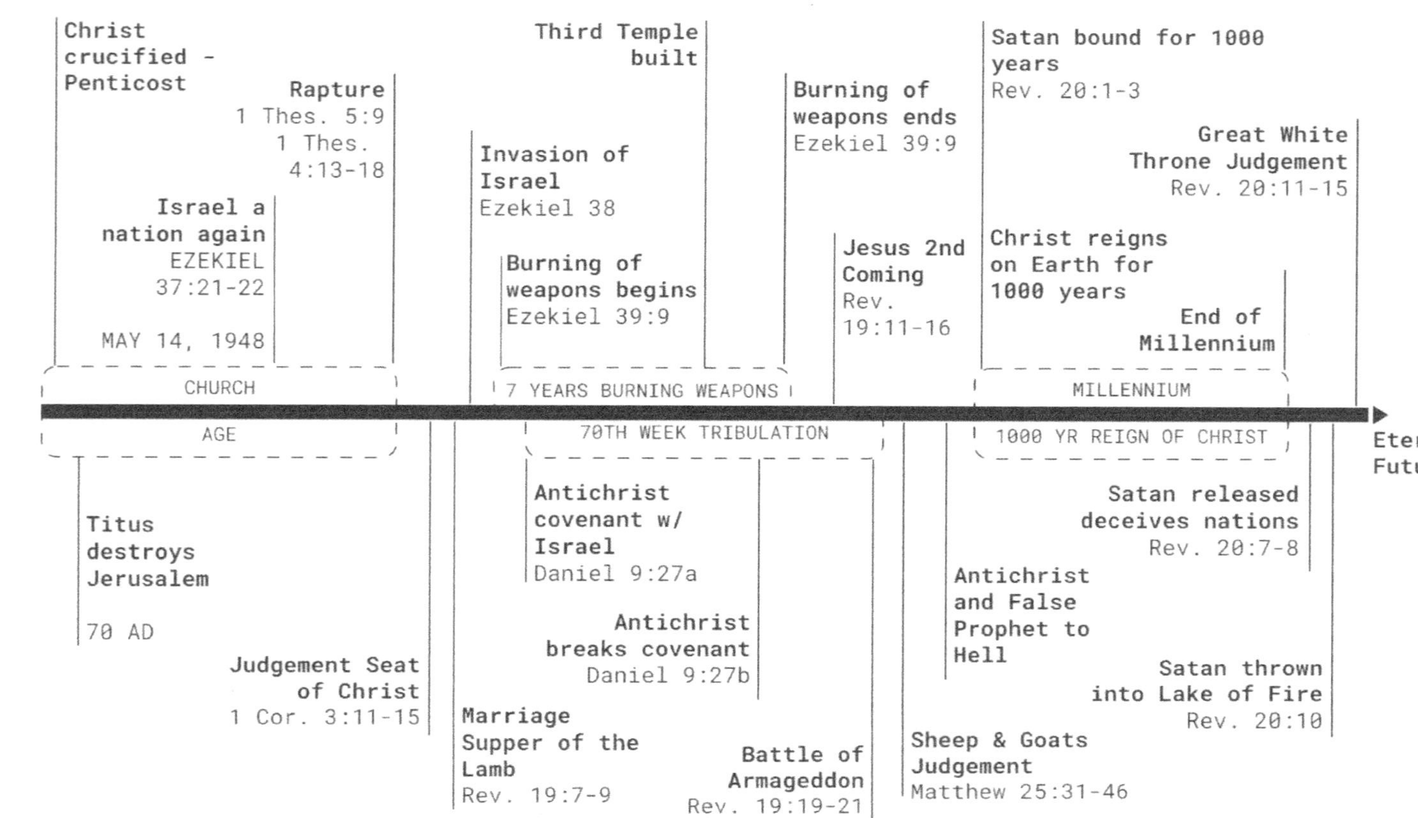

CHAPTER 1: WHY WE CAN TRUST THE BIBLE

Since we will be studying prophecy in the Bible, can we trust that what the Bible claims is true? If we cannot, we are wasting our time and we should be doing something more productive. But, if what the Bible says is true, then there is no other endeavor on earth that is more important. No one understands everything in the Bible, but what we can understand, we can trust that it is true-rock solid!

Some believe that parts are true and other sections are not. The problem with this thinking is the question-which parts? Either it is 100% true or we cannot trust any of it. Neither can we pick out the parts we like as true, but the rest is false because we do not like it. We cannot have a designer Bible any more than we can have a designer God.

The Bible is truth and truth does not go away. Jesus said in Matthew 24:35:

> *"Heaven and earth will pass away, but My words will by no means pass away."*

Peter wrote in 1 Peter 1:24-25:

> *"All flesh is as grass, and all the glory of man as the flower of the grass. The grass withers, and its flower falls away, but the word of the Lord endures forever"*.

The Bible was written over a period of 1500 years by 40 different men from all walks of life. Some would argue that with that many writers over that period of time, there would have to be some discrepancies. Paul wrote in 2 Timothy 3:16-17:

> *"All Scripture is given by inspiration of God, and is profitable for doctrine, for reproof, for correction, for instruction in righteousness, that the man of God may be complete, thoroughly equipped for every good work."*

The Bible was written by 40 different individuals, but only one author, the third Person of the Trinity, the Holy Spirit. Reading the Bible is one way that God communicates with people. Hebrews 4:12 says:

> *"For the Word of God is living and powerful, and sharper than any two-edged sword, piercing even to the division of soul and spirit, and of joints and marrow, and is a discerner of the thoughts and intents of the heart."*

We can have a fresh word from God every time we open it that speaks to our present situation. God loves us and He wants us to know more about Him. We can become better acquainted with Him through the pages of the Bible.

But, how can we know that the Bible has not been corrupted because it has been copied so many times? Wouldn't it be like the game "Gossip" where the final version of the original statement is completely different? Modern translations are made from original Hebrew, Greek and Aramaic source texts based on thousands of ancient manuscripts. In other words, each new copy that was made was taken from an original manuscript, not from another copy. Scribes that copied these manuscripts not only counted the words while they wrote, but also letters. If an error was detected, they would destroy the inaccurate copy and start over.

The Dead Sea Scrolls were found in the late 1940's near the Dead Sea in Israel. These scrolls were placed in jars and hidden in caves in that area. It is believed that they were placed there to preserve them before the Romans destroyed Israel in 70 AD. When comparing these ancient scrolls to the Bible we have today, the variations are miniscule!

We can be sure that the Bibles we have today are entirely accurate and reliable. God wants us to know Him exactly as He is. We can read our Bible and trust that it reflects the true nature of God.

The big question in our culture today is "Are the Bible's claims true?" Two-thirds of Americans say there is no such thing as absolute truth. Now it is generally believed that everyone can have their own "truth." And, what is true for you may not be true for me! Many people believe that there is more than one way to God, but Jesus said, *"I am **the Way, the Truth** and **the Life**, no man comes to the Father except by Me!"* Some would say that if you sincerely believe something about God, He will have to let you into heaven no matter what the Bible says. Jesus, Who is the Truth, wants us to know that He is the only Way as the Bible teaches.

But deep down, most people want the truth. That is why we have instant replays at football games. And, we would really be concerned if our pharmacist gave us a different drug then our doctor prescribed with the explanation, "All medicines are about the same. What's true for the doctor isn't necessarily true for me!" It is comforting to know that the Word of God that we rest our eternity on is completely accurate and true.

CHAPTER 2: WHY STUDY PROPHECY?

Prophecy never came by the will of man, but holy men of God spoke as they were moved by the Holy Spirit.

2 Peter 1:21.

Prophecy in the Bible has always interested many people. Just knowing what will happen in the future is exciting-even entertaining. Down through history, misguided individuals have predicted the second coming of Christ, but those "prophecies" were always wrong. As 2 Peter 1:21 says, prophecies were made by Holy men as they were moved by the Holy Spirit, so it wasn't man that was prophesying, but God was telling writers of the Bible through the Holy Spirit what would take place in the future. The study of prophecy should not be used for entertainment or profit, but because it is the Word of God and Christians can see prophecy that has been fulfilled and can read in the Bible of things to come. There are several reasons to study prophecy:

1. Fulfilled prophecy builds our faith. When we read what the prophets of old wrote thousands of years ago and see them fulfilled many years later, we can be sure that the unfulfilled prophecies will also be fulfilled. God is fulfilling prophecies that were written thousands of

years ago right before our very eyes today. When we see this happening, we can only stand in awe of our sovereign God.

2. The Bible teaches that there will be the Rapture and after that the Judgement Seat of Christ. This Judgement will be for Christians and is not to determine who goes to Heaven or Hell, but it is when Christ will judge the believers' works while they lived on the earth. (1 Cor 3:11-15). Knowing that all believers will stand before Christ to have their works judged for rewards should give them the encouragement to live Holy lives.

3. The apostle John prophesied in Revelation 20:11-14 that all people who reject Jesus Christ as their Savior will be judged at the Great White Throne of Judgement by none other than the One whom they rejected. This should give all Christians the motivation to share the Gospel with the lost, so that they won't have to experience the horrors of eternal hell.

4. As Christians study and understand prophecy they will have confidence in knowing that our God is the Sovereign One of the universe. We can know that He has our lives in His hands and that when things seem the worst, He is still in control. We can have His peace in the midst of the turmoil of the last days.

Does the fact that Jesus' Second Coming was prophesied so many years ago make you wonder if He will ever return? Why or why not?

Does what Jesus said about the days of Noah in Matthew 24:36-39 change the way you think about the Rapture?

If you really believed that He could return at any time, would the way you are living now change in any way?

CHAPTER 3: THE FIRST SIN

Then God saw everything that He had made, and indeed it was very good. So, the evening and the morning were the sixth day.

Genesis 1:31

And out of the ground the Lord God made every tree grow that is pleasant to the sight and good for food. The tree of life was also in the midst of the garden, and the tree of the knowledge of good and evil.

Genesis 2:9

For six days our Creator God made the universe and everything in it. On the evening of the sixth day He declared that all He had made was "very good." Lastly, He created man to care for the Garden of Eden where God had placed him. It was Adam's job to tend the garden and to name all the living creatures that God brought to him.

Within the garden, God made every tree that was pleasant to the eye and good for food. Among those trees were two special trees: the tree of life and the tree of the knowledge of good and evil. The tree of life sustained Adam and Eve's lives and had the ability to prolong their lives forever.

But the fruit of the tree of the knowledge of good and evil was forbidden by God. One might call this tree the tree of total knowledge. This fruit provided man with the ability to decide what he believed was best for him, apart from God. God warned Adam (and after she was created, Adam warned Eve):

> *Of every tree of the garden you may freely eat; but of the tree of the knowledge of good and evil you shall not eat, for in the day that you eat of it you shall surely die.*
>
> *Genesis 2:16-17.*

At that point, Satan in the form of a serpent, came to tempt Eve. Satan used the same method to tempt Eve to sin as he does us today. He said to Eve, *"Has God indeed said, 'You shall not eat of every tree of the garden'?"* Asking this question put doubt in Eve's mind concerning God's ways and goodness of character. Satan's goal was to make Eve think that God was not protecting her and Adam from harm but was in fact withholding a good thing from them. So, she was led to believe that it was God that was selfish because He would not allow them to be like Himself. She was experiencing the good of her environment, but she wanted more-she wanted to have knowledge of the evil.

Through the ages, Satan has tempted mankind by making them believe that God is withholding pleasure from them. Just as God created the Garden for man's good, he also created sex so that men and women could experience pleasure, **but only within**

the bounds of marriage. The sexual revolution of the 60's is an example of people believing that they know better than God. It was like Satan was (and is) saying to us, "Did God indeed say that sex should only be between a man and a woman who are married? God is being selfish with you. He is keeping you from enjoying sex with whoever you want. There are no consequences. He will not punish you. You will not surely die." People believed that lie and they still do. As a result, much suffering and misery has come upon our society and world. Paul in Romans 16:19 wrote, *"be wise in what is good, and innocent in what is evil."* Sometimes ignorance is a good thing, especially ignorance of various forms of evil. Eve wanted to know about both good and evil and because of Adam's and her sin, the world has suffered, and all mankind possesses a sin nature.

Watchman Nee wrote, "Since the day that Adam took the fruit of the tree of knowledge (of good and evil), man has been engaged in deciding what is good and what is evil."

Now this generation celebrates its debauchery by encouraging the next generation to go deeper into evil. Jesus warned us about causing "little ones to sin."

But whoever causes one of these little ones who believe in Me to sin, it would be better for him if a millstone were hung around his neck, and he were drowned in the depth of the sea.

Matthew 18:6

Instead of going to God and confessing their sin, Adam and Eve hid from Him. He had to find them. For the first time they recognized that they were naked and made coverings of fig leaves. Fig leaves were not good enough to cover Adam and Eve's nakedness. It took the skin of an animal that God provided to do the job. This was the first sacrifice for sin in the scriptures.

Without the shedding of blood there can be no forgiveness of sin.

Hebrews 9:22.

God does not let sin go unpunished. For the serpent, God made him crawl on his belly in the dust all the days of his life. Also, He put enmity between the serpent and the woman and between her Seed and the serpent's seed. Her Seed would bruise his head and his seed will bruise her Seed's heel.

Our God wants peace and fellowship with the people He created. When Adam and Eve sinned (and He knew they would), He had a plan to bring mankind back into precious fellowship with Himself. God did not say that his Seed would bruise Satan's head, but **her** seed would. It would be Mary's Seed that would be our Savior. This is the first reference to the virgin birth. Mary was Jesus' mother, but God was His Father. He was fully human and fully God. God's Son was the only perfect Man that ever lived and so He was the only one who could be the perfect sacrifice for the whole world.

PROPHECIES MADE	PROPHECIES FULFILLED
Genesis 3:15	Luke 23:33, Luke 24:6
God put enmity between Satan and Christ Mary's Seed	Jesus is Mary's Seed, not Joseph's First reference to the Virgin Birth
Satan would bruise Christ's heel	Jesus suffered on the cross
Jesus would crush Satan's head	Jesus rose from the dead on the third day defeating Satan forever

Many believe that God gives us "rules" to prevent us from having a "good time." How do His commandments show His love for us?

Adam and Eve fashioned fig leaves to cover their nakedness. Because the fig leaves did not suffice in covering their sin, God brought them an animal's skin to replace the fig leaves. How did that act prophesy our Savior's death on the cross?

Jesus was prophesied to be Mary's Son by the Holy Spirit. Why was it vital that Jesus be God's Son and not Joseph's?

CHAPTER 4: ABRAHAM-THE FATHER OF ISRAEL

Now the Lord had said to Abram: "Get out of your country, from your family and from your father's house, to a land that I will show you. I will make you a great nation; I will bless you and make your name great; and you shall be a blessing. I will bless those who bless you, and I will curse him who curses you; and in you all the families of the earth shall be blessed.

Genesis 12:1-3

Abraham was born in the city of Ur of the Chaldeans. God's command was for him to leave his country, his tribe and his family and move to a place that He would show him. For a man of Abraham's stature, this kind of move was unheard of. Hebrews 11:8 teaches that it was "by faith" that Abraham obeyed not knowing where he was going.

Abraham's faith in God prompted him to go as God had instructed. He believed that what God promises, He will do. His faith in God was evident in his *willingness* to obey God.

There were seven elements to God's promise to Abraham.

1. God promised to create "a great nation" through Abraham.
2. God promised to bless Abraham.
3. Abraham's "name" would live on after his lifetime.
4. Abraham was commanded "to be a blessing" to others.
5. God would "bless those who bless" Abraham (Israel).
6. God would "curse those who curse Abraham (Israel).
7. All the families of the earth would be blessed through Abraham and his descendants.

Abraham's descendants were the nation of Israel. One can sum up God's promises into three parts. God promised Abraham the "**Land**," which is the Nation of Israel; the "**Seed**" is the people (Abraham's descendants) that make up that Nation; and the **"Blessing"** Who is none other than the Savior of the world-Jesus Christ and the Word of God which is our Bible.

The nation of Israel is the apple of God's eye. He chose them because He loved them and it was His choice.

For you are a holy people to the Lord your God; the Lord your God has chosen you to be a people for Himself, a special treasure above all the peoples on the face of the earth. The Lord did not set His love on you nor choose you because you were more in number than any other people, for you were the least of all peoples; but because the Lord loves you and **because He would keep the oath which He swore to your fathers***…*

Deuteronomy 7:6-8a.

Down through the ages since God gave Abraham these promises, God has punished nations that have "cursed" (could be translated "disdained") his nation, Israel. Disdain means the feeling that someone (or some people) is unworthy of one's consideration or respect, having an attitude of contempt toward a people or nation. Even just disdain for the Jewish nation would provoke God's judgement. Abraham descendants, the Jews, have been a great spiritual blessing to all the nations of the world. God, through the Jews, has given us His Word, the Bible, and our Savior, Jesus. Because of this, all nations should "bless" Israel, but most disdain her. Stephen J. Bramer, Dallas Theological Seminary Professor wrote: *"Why is there suffering in the world? One answer is that some people and nations have chosen not to bless Abraham and his descendants."*

God was very serious when he promised to bless the nations that bless Israel and curse the nations that disdain her.

PROPHECIES MADE	PROPHECIES FULFILLED
Genesis 12:1-2 God promised Abram Land, Seed, and blessing to all nations	Land-The Land of Israel Seed-The Jewish People Blessing-Our Savior Jesus Christ
Deuteronomy 7:6-8a Abram's descendants, the Jews, would be God's chosen people	Romans 11:1-5 The Jews continue to be His chosen people
Genesis 12:3 God promised to bless those who bless Israel and curse those who curse Israel	God has fulfilled his promises God has blessed the USA for treating Israel well and cursed many nations for treating them badly.

To move from where he was established in Ur of the Chaldeans at age 75 must have taken Abraham out of his comfort zone. Humanly speaking, it didn't make sense. Do you believe God could ever command you to do something that would take you out of your comfort zone? Why or why not?

What nations of the world disdained Israel and what were the results?

What nations of the world blessed Israel and what were the results?

CHAPTER 5: IS ISRAEL STILL GOD'S CHOSEN PEOPLE?

*And the Lord said to Abram…"Lift your eyes now and look from the place where you are- northward, southward, eastward, and westward; for all the land which you see I give to you and your descendants **forever**. And I will make your descendants as the dust of the earth; so that if a man could number the dust of the earth, then your descendants also could be numbered."*

Genesis 13:14-16.

One of the most disturbing trends in many churches and denominations today is the popularity of an amillennial interpretation of the promises God made to Abraham. Dr. Thomas Constable, pastor and former professor at Dallas Theological Seminary, wrote in his Notes on Genesis, page 197: "*The amillennial interpretation of this promise is that it "does not pertain today to unbelieving, ethnic 'Israel' but to Jesus Christ and his church." This interpretation applies the promise to the spiritual seed of Abraham (Christians), but not to the physical seed (Jews). However, there is no reason for accepting this more obscure explanation. Abraham understood the promise as applying to his physical descendants, and later revelation encourages us to understand it this way too.*"

God repeated these promises in Genesis not only to Abram (later, God changed his name to Abraham), (Gen 17:1-8) but also to his son, Isaac, (Gen 26:2-5) and his grandson, Jacob (Gen 28:12-15). Hank Hanegraaff, the radio talk show host of "Bible Answer Man" has written, *"The covenant between God and Israel (Abram's descendants) was broken with the rejection of His Son."* Hank forgot or didn't recognize that **God's promise was forever**, and it was not a bi-lateral promise (a promise or covenant that is valid only if both parties comply), but a unilateral (unconditional) promise (a promise or covenant that is valid no matter what the other party does).

In chapter 15 of Genesis, God reinforced His unconditional promises to Abram. Abram was getting up in years as was his wife Sarah, both past childbearing years. God confirmed that "one from his own body would be his heir." Then God took him outside and showed him the stars and proclaimed to Abram, "So shall your descendants be." He also said that the land where he was living would be his inheritance. Abram asked, "Lord God, how shall I know that I will inherit it?" To answer Abram's question, God instructed him to cut some animals into two pieces and lay the pieces opposite of each other so the blood would drain to the middle. When the sun was going down, Abram fell into a deep sleep. When it was dark, there appeared a "smoking oven and a burning torch" that passed between those pieces. The "smoking oven and a burning torch were symbols of God walking through the pieces. Abram did not walk through the pieces, only God alone.

A note in the Jeremiah Study Bible, page 23, helps us to understand what happened in verses 15:7-12 and 17:

To establish and confirm a covenant in Abram's day, usually the two parties would walk between the pieces of the sacrificial animals, saying, in effect, "May what has happened to these creatures happen to me if I break the covenant." The Hebrew expression "to cut a covenant" pertains to the act of cutting the sacrificial animals in two (Gen 15:18). Because this was Yahweh's (God's) sovereign covenant with Abram, not an agreement between equals, symbols of God (a smoking oven and a burning torch) passed between those pieces; Abram did not. The Lord made the covenant with no conditions-independent of Abram-and He would fulfill it in His time.

In Genesis, chapter 17 the Lord again appeared to Abram when he was 99 years old. It was at this time that God changed his name from Abram, meaning "exalted father," to Abraham meaning "father of a multitude." God again spelled out the terms of this unilateral covenant, now called the **Abrahamic Covenant**. God told him again that He would multiply him exceedingly (17:2), he would become the father of many nations (17:4), this would be an **everlasting** covenant to Abraham and his descendants (17:7) and He gave Abraham and his descendants after him all the land of Canaan as an **everlasting** possession (17:8).

The emphasis must be put on the truth that this was an unconditional, unilateral promise that God made to Abraham. There were no conditions that Abraham or the Jewish nation had to keep for this covenant to remain valid. God knew that the Jews would forsake their God many times down through history even to the point of rejecting His Son. Make no mistakes about it, the Jews as a nation paid for their sins against God. He severely disciplined them time and again, but He never forsook them, and He never quit loving them. Probably no prophet said this better than Jeremiah:

> *"Therefore do not fear, O My servant Jacob," says the Lord, "Nor be dismayed, O Israel: For behold, I will save you from afar, and your seed from the land of their captivity. Jacob shall return, have rest and be quiet, and no one shall make him afraid. For I am with you," says the Lord, "to save you; though I make a full end of all nations where I have scattered you, **yet I will not make a complete end of you, But I will correct you in justice and will not let you go altogether unpunished**."*

> *Jeremiah 30:10-11.*

Jesus, as He came to Jerusalem on a donkey, knew that he would be rejected and crucified. As He entered, He wept over the city. He could look ahead to 70 AD when Titus, the Roman general would destroy the city and the Jews that were not killed would be dispersed to many nations and would not return as a nation until May 14, 1948 as was prophesied in Jeremiah:

> *"Therefore, behold, the days are coming," says the Lord, "that they shall no longer say, 'As the Lord lives who brought up the children of Israel from the land of Egypt,' "but, 'As the Lord lives who brought up and led the descendants of the house of Israel from the north country and from all the countries where I had driven them.' And they shall dwell in their own land."*
>
> *Jeremiah 23:7-8*

If there was ever a situation when it would seem right for God to renege on his promise to Abraham and his descendants, it would be when they crucified His Son. But God is faithful, and He keeps his promises. One cannot overemphasize the importance of understanding that the Abrahamic Covenant is an unconditional, unilateral covenant between God and the Jews. As was stated earlier, many churches and denominations in the 21st century either don't understand this fact or they choose not to. If they did believe it, it would be impossible for them to say that the Israel we know today is just another secular nation (or worse) and not the precious land that God had promised to Abraham and his descendants. The Jews are still God's chosen people!

There is a strong correlation between God's choosing the Jews and choosing us as Christians:

1. God chose Israel-God chose us.
2. God gave the land to Israel; they didn't earn it-God has given us a heavenly land we didn't earn.
3. God promised that the Jews would be God's chosen people forever-God promised us that we are forever His.
4. Even though God disciplined Israel for their sin, he never took away their land-As Christians, God disciplines us when we sin, but we still belong to Him and He will not take away our Heavenly land.
5. It was through Israel that the blessing of Jesus came to the whole world-It is through Christians that the Holy Spirit works to bless others as we share Jesus them.

PROPHECIES MADE	PROPHECIES FULFILLED
Genesis 15:4-5 God promised Abram a son	Genesis 21:1-3 Sarah bore Abraham a son-Isaac
Genesis 12:7 & Genesis 13:14-15 God Promised Abram's descendants land	May 14, 1948 Israel became a nation again
Genesis 12:3b In Abraham all the families of the earth would be blessed	Luke 2:6-7 Mary, a virgin, bore the Savior of the world

QUESTIONS FOR DISCUSSION

Why have many churches have rejected the idea that Israel is still God's chosen people?

Why do you think that God repeatedly proclaimed that He gave the land to Abraham's descendants forever? What action did He take to show He was serious?

Why is it so important to the world's nations that they treat Israel with respect and bless them?

CHAPTER 6: FOUR HUNDRED YEARS IN EGYPT

Now when the sun was going down, a deep sleep fell upon Abram; and behold horror and great darkness fell upon him. Then He (God) said to Abram: "Know certainly that your descendants will be strangers in a land that is not theirs, and will serve them, and they will afflict them for four hundred years. And also, the nation whom they serve I will judge; afterward, they shall come out with great possessions. Now as for you, you shall go to your fathers in peace; you shall be buried at a good old age. But in the fourth generation they shall return here, for the iniquity of the Amorites is not yet complete."

Genesis 15:12-16

While God promised Abram that he would inherit the land of Israel (**the Abrahamic Covenant**), He also foretold that his descendants would be enslaved in Egypt for 400 years. Joseph, one of Jacob's son (and Abraham's great grandson) was sold into slavery by his brothers and was taken to Egypt. Through a series of miraculous events, Joseph became the second ruler of Egypt just under the Pharaoh. God instructed him to have the people store most of the grain produced for seven years because He was going to send a drought for the next seven years. Because of the stored grain, the Egyptian people survived during the drought. The drought not only covered Egypt, but also Canaan where Joseph's father Jacob and his brothers remained. Jacob heard about the grain in Egypt and told Joseph's ten brothers (all but Benjamin) to go to Egypt and buy grain so they could survive the famine.

Joseph's brothers brought back grain to their father in Canaan. Not knowing that they were dealing with their brother, they came back to Egypt to buy more grain. Finally, after Joseph was satisfied that his brothers were sorry that they had sold him into slavery, he revealed to them who he was. Joseph showed his brothers unbelievable grace and invited his whole family to move down to Egypt where they settled.

Jacob and his family moved to Egypt in 1875 BC. Thirty years later the population of Jacob's family had grown so much that the next Pharaoh (who did not know Joseph) was worried that if Egypt got in a war, the descendants of Abraham might join with Egypt's enemies. So, the new Pharaoh enslaved God's people in the year 1845 BC. When the 400 years were about to come to an end, God called Moses to rescue His people. As he called Moses to that task, He also confirmed His covenant with Abraham.

*And God spoke to Moses and said to him: "I am the Lord. I appeared to Abraham, to Isaac and to Jacob, as God Almighty, but by My name Lord I was not known to them. I have also established My covenant (**the Abrahamic Covenant**) with them, to give them the land of Canaan, the land of their pilgrimage, in which they were strangers. And I have also heard the groaning of the children of Israel whom the Egyptians keep in bondage, and I have remembered My covenant.*

Exodus 6:2-5

In order to get Pharaoh's "attention," God sent a series of judgements upon the whole nation of Egypt to encourage Pharaoh to let God's people go. The 10th and last judgement was the most severe for the Egyptians. It meant the death of every first-born of every Egyptian family from Pharaoh's to the lowliest family including the livestock. To protect that plague from causing death to the Israelite families, God provided a way that he would protect them from the plague that the Egyptians would experience.

God instructed each Jewish family to obtain a year-old male lamb without blemish. (Exodus 12:5) On the 14th day of the month at twilight they were told to kill the lamb and take some of its blood to sprinkle on the two doorposts and the lintel of their house. Then they were to roast the lamb and eat it hurriedly. At midnight God passed through the land of Egypt and struck down the first-born of every Egyptian family, but when He saw the blood on the doorposts and lintels of the Israelite's houses, He "passed over" their homes so they were not harmed. The next day Pharaoh allowed God's people to leave Egypt.

God instructed the people to memorialize that event and to this day "Passover" is celebrated by Jewish families throughout the world. To the Christians, it has an even deeper meaning. Our **perfect Lamb of God,** Jesus, was slain on the cross. His precious blood was shed for us that we also might not die but have eternal life. St Peter put it this way:

> *"...knowing that you were not redeemed with corruptible things, like silver or gold, from your aimless conduct received by tradition from your father, but with the precious blood of Christ, as of a lamb without blemish and without spot."*
>
> *1 Peter 1:18-19*

After the final judgement of death to Egypt's firstborns sent by God, Pharaoh finally let the people go. In 1446 BC, Moses led the people out of Egypt. Just as God promised Abraham, their slavery ended in the fourth generation (a generation in those days was considered to be 100 year) and **they left with much wealth from the Egyptians.**

"And I (God) will give this people (the Israelites) favor in the sight of the Egyptians; and it shall be, when you go, that you shall not go empty-handed. But every woman shall ask of her neighbor, namely, of her who dwells near her house, articles of silver, articles of gold, and clothing; and you shall put them on your sons and on your daughters. So, you shall plunder the Egyptians."

Exodus 3:21-22

"Speak now in the hearing of the people, and let every man ask from his neighbor and every woman from her neighbor, articles of silver and articles of gold." And the Lord gave the people favor in the sight of the Egyptians. Moreover, the man Moses was very great in the land of Egypt, and the sight of Pharaoh's servants and in the sight of the people.

Exodus 11:2-3

And the Lord had given the people favor in the sight of the Egyptians, so that they granted them what they requested. Thus, they plundered the Egyptians.

Exodus 12:36

God had turned the hearts of the common Egyptian people toward the people of Israel and they gave them great wealth. Thomas Constable, former professor at Dallas Theological Seminary, on page 98 of his Notes on Exodus wrote:

> *The Israelites "asked" the Egyptians to give them the articles mentioned, not to lend them with a view to getting them back. The Israelites, from this time on until they left Egypt, received many such gifts from the Egyptians-enough to build the tabernacle, its furniture, furnishings, and utensils, as well as the priests' garments. This reflects the respect and fear the Israelites enjoyed in Egypt following these plagues.*

God had proven once again that the people of Israel were His chosen by providing everything they would need when they left Egypt. He did so just as He had promised Abraham that He would 535 year before. He is still a caring God who supplies for all our needs as Christians. He showed repeatedly his love for the Jewish people and He showed us proof of His love through the precious sacrifice of His Son for the forgiveness of our sins.

PROPHECIES MADE	PROPHECIES FULFILLED
Genesis 15:12-16 The Israelites would be slaves in Egypt for 400 years	Exodus 1:7-11 The Egyptians enslaved the Jews for 400
Genesis 15:12-16 The Israelites would leave with wealth	Exodus 12:36 With the gifts they received, they plundered Egypt

QUESTIONS FOR DISCUSSION

Why did "horror and great darkness" fall upon Abraham when he was in a deep sleep?

How did Joseph, Egypt's "Secretary of Agriculture," protect Abraham's blessing to the world?

Does it seem strange to you that the Egyptian people would give the Israelites expensive gifts while they were slaves? Why would they do such a thing? Why would the Israelites need these gifts?

God prophesied to Abraham 535 years before that the Israelites would need these gifts. Do you believe that God knows what you will need in the future? Do you think He will provide them for you?

How is the lamb's blood on the doorposts and lintel a symbol of what Jesus did for us on the cross?

CHAPTER 7: THE DAVIDIC COVENANT

After the Israelites left Egypt, God had commanded them to enter the promised land (Canaan). Twelve men were instructed to go into the land to spy it out. They were to see what the people and the land was like. When they returned, only Joshua and Caleb were optimistic about the Israelites being able to defeat the Canaanites who dwelt there. The other ten reported that it couldn't be done. They forgot that God told them to go and He would fight for them and they would win and take the land that God had given them. Because of their unbelief God disciplined them by making them wander in the wilderness for forty years until everyone over twenty years old had died. The only exceptions were Caleb, Joshua and Moses.

The Israelites entered the promised land in the year 1406 BC. They drove out most of the pagan inheritance. They had a theocracy (ruled by God) until the people cried out for a king so they could be like all the other nations around them. The prophet Samuel warned them that God would not be pleased, and they would pay a price for disobeying God. But the people still wanted a king. Saul was chosen to be the first king of Israel in 1051 BC and reigned for 40 years. He was followed by David who reigned for 40 and one-half years when he turned the kingdom over to his son, Solomon in 971 BC.

David, although certainly not perfect, was a good king. He was called "a man after God's own heart." He had some grievous sins in his reign which cost him and his people dearly. But David loved God and when the Lord *"gave him rest from all his enemies"* David said to Nathan, the prophet:

> *"See how, I dwell in a house of cedar, but the ark of God dwells inside tent curtains." Then Nathan said to the King, "Go, do all that is in your heart for the Lord is with you."*
>
> *2 Samuel 7:2-3.*

That night, the word of the Lord came to Nathan saying that David should **not** build a temple for the Lord. God gave three reasons why he shouldn't:

1.	There was no pressing need to do so since the ark had resided in tents since the Exodus. 2 Samuel 7:6

2.	God had not commanded his people to build a permanent temple. 2 Samuel 7:7

3.	David had much blood on his hands, since he was a man of war. 1 Chronicles 22:8

God through Nathan reminded David that He was the One who took him from following his sheep to be ruler of Israel. Plus, He had been with him wherever he had gone and had given him victory over all his enemies. Furthermore, He had given him a great name. 2 Samuel 7:8-9.

When God through Nathan told David that he would not be the one to build a temple, He laid out what He **would** do for him in the future. These promises are called the **Davidic Covenant**. Like the Abrahamic Covenant, the Davidic Covenant was given as an unconditional covenant. It in some ways gave more detail to the Abrahamic Covenant, especially details that have to do with his house or dynasty that would be eternal. The final ruler will be Jesus who will rule forever. Praise His Holy Name!

> *"Moreover, I will appoint a place for My people Israel, and will plant them, that they may dwell in a place of their own and **move no more**; nor shall the sons of wickedness oppress them anymore as previously."*
>
> *2 Samuel 7:10*

Since God has brought the Jewish people back from the nations of the world and Israel is a State again, that nation will never again cease to exist. That part of the Davidic Covenant in my view has been fulfilled. But the second part of that verse will not be fulfilled until Jesus reigns from Jerusalem, during the thousand-year reign of our Savior when He returns.

> *"When your days are fulfilled and you rest with your father, I will set up your seed (Solomon-Jesus) after you, who will come from your*

*body, and I will establish his kingdom. He shall
build a house (temple-dynasty) for My name,
and I will establish the throne (right to rule) of
his kingdom forever."*

2 Samuel 7:12

God promised David that it would be his seed,
Solomon, that would build the temple and his rule
would be established. Ultimately, however, David's
"Seed" would be the Messiah Jesus and His rule
(dynasty) will be eternal.

*"I will be his Father, and he shall be My son. If
he commits iniquity, I will chasten him with the
rod of men and with the blows of the sons of
men. But My mercy shall not depart from him,
as I took it from Saul, whom I removed from
before you."*

2 Samuel 7:14-15

God went on to speak about Solomon's rule of Israel.
It would be like a Father-son relationship, but if
Solomon committed sin (which he did), God would
discipline him severely. However, God's mercy
would never depart from him. This again is an
example of God's unconditional promise that would
never be taken away no matter what Israel or its
rulers did.

*"And your house (dynasty) and your kingdom
shall be established **forever** before you. Your*

throne (right to rule) shall be established ***forever**.*

2 Samuel 7:16

It is human nature for people to want something good in their lives that will keep on giving after their lives on earth cease. God promised David just such a thing on steroids. Verse 16 is a wonderful promise to David that his dynasty would continue forever, and the last King would be the Messiah Himself. What a thrill it must have been to hear from God through the mouth of Nathan that David would be the first king of a dynasty that would last eternally. Most peoples' names are remembered for only a generation or two after their death. But David's name is remembered today through the pages of the Bible and will be forever remembered because of the unconditional covenant God made with him. In the passage that follows (2 Samuel 7:16-29), David humbly expressed his sincere gratitude to God for the grace and honor He bestowed on him.

"Therefore, You are great, O Lord God. For there is none like You, nor is there any God besides You, according to all that we have heard with our ears. And who is like Your people, like Israel, the one nation on the earth whom God went to redeem for Himself as a people, to make for Himself a name-and to do for Yourself great and awesome deeds for Your land-before Your people whom You

God, however, did not promise that the rule of
David's descendants would be without interruption.
The Babylonian captivity, the destruction of Israel in
70 AD and the dispersion of the Jews are clear
examples of this interruption. But the privilege of
ruling over Israel **as king** would always belong to
David's descendants. Israel's next King will be the
King of Kings-King Jesus when He returns at His
Second Advent.

There are five major implications of the Davidic Covenant for the future:

1. God must preserve the Jewish people as a nation. (Fulfilled)
2. He must bring them back into their land. (Fulfilled 1948)
3. A descendant of David (Jesus Christ) must rule over them in the land of Israel. (To be fulfilled during the Millennium)
4. His kingdom must be an earthly kingdom, as opposed to a spiritual rule from Heaven. (To be fulfilled during the Millennium)
5. This kingdom must be everlasting. (To be fulfilled during the Millennium and the new Heaven and Earth)

"This covenant, let it be most definitely understood, has to do with a literal posterity, and a literal throne, and a literal kingdom. To start 'spiritualizing it into meaning a heavenly posterity and a spiritual kingdom synonymous with the Christian Church is to violate the very first principle of Scripture interpretation, namely, the principle that plainly spoken words should at least be accepted as meaning what they say."

J. Sidlow Baxter, a pastor and author, quote taken from his book "Explore the Book."

The Davidic Covenant is the fourth major development in Messianic prophecy. The others including the fourth include:

First, in Genesis 3:14-15, God promised that the Seed of the woman (Jesus) will bruise the head of the serpent (Satan's). Jesus would come through **the human race**. He had to be born of a virgin, be a human and live a perfect life to be a perfect sacrifice for us.

Second, in Genesis 12:2-3, God promised Abraham that He shall be a blessing and in him all the nations of the world be blessed. The blessing was Jesus. Since Abraham was the father of the Jews, Jesus would come through **the nation of Israel.**

Third, in Genesis 49:10, God speaking through Jacob to his son Judah, "the scepter (the right to rule) would not depart from the tribe of Judah…. until Shiloh (Bearer of Rest, who is Jesus) shall come." **Judah is the tribe** from where Jesus, the Blessing, would come.

Fourth, in 2 Samuel 7:16, God speaking through Nathan, prophesied that the blessing (Jesus) would come from the **family of David**.

Fifth, in Luke 1:26-27, God sent the angel Gabriel to Mary, a virgin, who was of the house of David and announced to her that she would conceive in her womb and bring forth a Son, and she would call His name Jesus. The blessing would come through **a person, the virgin Mary**.

PROPHECIES MADE	PROPHECIES FULFILLED
2 Samuel 7:10 Israelites would have a place and move no more.	May 14, 1948 Israel again becomes a nation in the land that God promised
2 Samuel 7:12 God promised David his son Solomon would build the temple.	1 Kings 6:14 Solomon finished building the temple.
2 Samuel 7:14-15 If Israel disobeyed God, He would discipline them.	2 Kings 25:8-11 Jerusalem and Temple destroyed; people taken captive
2 Samuel 7:16 Jesus, David's seed will rule in Jerusalem forever.	Yet to be fulfilled

Why is it that usually God asks us to do something that we can't do in our own strength?

When we are faithful to obey God, what effect does it have on those around us?

Have you ever wanted to do "something for God" and God said "No"? How did that make you feel? Did God steer you in a different direction? What did you learn from that experience?

Both Saul (the first King of Israel) and David (the second King of Israel) sinned against God. How were their responses different when confronted about their sins? Compare 1 Samuel 13:8-14 vs. 2 Samuel 12:1-15. How did their responses change history? What lesson does that teach us about dealing with our sins?

CHAPTER 8: SOLOMON-THE WISEST MAN THAT EVER LIVED

Before King David died, he charged his son saying:

> *"I go the way of all the earth; be strong, therefore, and prove yourself a man. And keep the charge of the Lord your God: to walk in His ways, to Keep His statutes, His commandments, His judgments, and His testimonies, as it is written in the Law of Moses, that you may prosper in all that you do and wherever you turn; that the Lord may fulfill His word which He spoke concerning me, saying, 'If your sons take heed to their way to walk before Me in truth with all their heart and with all their soul,' He said, 'you shall not lack a man on the throne of Israel.'*
>
> *1 Kings 2:2-4*

Solomon's reign as king began in the year 971 BC. First Kings 3:4 says that Solomon loved the Lord. God appeared to Solomon in a dream and he told Solomon to ask for anything and He would give it to him. Solomon asked for wisdom to rule God's chosen people-the Israelites. Because Solomon asked for wisdom, God not only gave him *"a wise and understanding heart, so that there has not been anyone like you before you nor shall any like you arise after you." (1 Kings 3:12),* but also riches and honor.

Solomon desired to build a house for the Lord, just as David had wanted to, but the Lord prevented David from building it. Solomon knew that God had told his father *"your son, whom I will set on your throne in your place, he shall build the house for My name." (1 Kings 5:5b)* So, in the year 966 BC, Solomon began building a temple for the Lord.

The temple was unbelievably beautiful. The dimensions were approximately 90 feet long, 30 feet wide and 45 feet high. It had about 2,700 square feet of floor space. Its exterior was limestone, cedar, and gold. The temple was small and was not designed for a congregation, so the congregation assembled in the large open courtyard.

When the outside of the temple was completed, the word of the Lord came to Solomon saying:

> *"Concerning this temple which you are building, if you walk in My statutes, execute My judgments, keep all My commandments, and walk in them, then I will perform My word with you, which I spoke to your father David. And I will dwell among the children of Israel and will not forsake My people Israel."*
>
> *1 Kings 6:12-13.*

It took Solomon seven and one-half years to complete the temple. When the temple was finished, the Lord again came to Solomon. God warned him a second time about the importance of following the commandments that He had given his father David. If he or his sons turned from following God but instead followed other gods, then He would cut off Israel from the land which He had given them, and the temple would be destroyed. 1 Kings 9:1-9.

The warning that Israel being "cut off" from the land if the people did not follow the Lord's commandments did not mean that the land would not still belong to the Jews. It meant that the people would be exiled for a time then God would bring them back to the land.

Many from the known world at that time learned of Solomon's great wisdom and wealth. First Kings 10 tells about the Queen of Sheba traveling 1,200 miles from what is now known as Yemen, to "test" Solomon's knowledge and to see the temple. She brought with her many gifts including 120 talents of Gold which would have the value today of $200 million. She was so impressed that she said to the King:

> *"It was a true report which I heard in my own land about your words and your wisdom. However, I did not believe the words until I came and saw with my own eyes; and indeed, the half was not told to me. Your wisdom and*

1 Kings 10:6-9

King Solomon had everything he could possibly want which included the one thing that God forbade him to have. The chink in Solomon's armor was foreign women. Solomon loved foreign women so much that he married 700 wives and had 300 concubines. God had prohibited Israelites from taking foreign women as wives. He said in 1 Kings 11:2b: *"You shall not intermarry with them, nor they with you. Surely they will turn away your hearts after their gods."* Solomon clung to these in love (or should we say lust?)

When Solomon was a young king, he had an undivided heart and loved God. His many wives caused him to have a divided heart and to please these foreign women, he built "high places" where children were sacrificed to their false gods. Because his heart was divided, God divided his Kingdom and, in His anger, told Solomon:

"Because you have done this and have not kept My covenant and My statutes, which I

have commanded you, I will surely tear the kingdom away from you and give it to your servant (Jeroboam). Nevertheless, I will not do it in your days, for the sake of your father David; I will tear it out of the hand of your son. However, I will not tear away the whole kingdom; I will give one tribe (Judah) to your son for the sake of my servant David, and for the sake of Jerusalem which I have chosen."

1 Kings 11:11-14.

After Solomon died in 931 BC, his kingdom was divided. Jeroboam ruled the northern kingdom (Israel) and Rehoboam, Solomon's son was king over the tribe of Judah, the southern kingdom. Later, the tribe of Benjamin was added to the southern kingdom. Judah was the tribe from which the Messiah was to come.

PROPHECIES MADE	PROPHECIES FULFILLED
I KINGS 3:12 God promised wisdom, riches & honor to Solomon.	I KINGS 10:6-9 Solomon was the richest & wisest man to ever live.
2 SAMUEL 7:12 God promised David that his son, Solomon, would build the temple.	I KINGS 6:14 Solomon finished building the Temple in the year 959 BC.

David and Solomon both began their years of ruling with full obedience and love for God and God blessed them beyond belief. Yet in their later years they became lax in their devotion to God and made huge blunders as Kings. What would cause them to commit such sins? Have we seen the same thing happen in our generation? Could this happen to us? If so, how can we prevent it? Is the saying true, "There's no fool like an old fool?" How can we finish our Christian lives well?

CHAPTER 9: EVENTS LEADING UP TO THE BABYLON CAPTIVITY

"Behold, I set before you today a blessing and a curse: the blessing, if you obey the commandments of the Lord your God which I command you today; and the curse, if you do not obey the commandments of the Lord your God, but turn aside from the way which I command you today, to go after other gods which you have not known."

Deuteronomy 11:26-28

After Solomon's death when Rehoboam, his son was king, Israel was divided. The northern kingdom was made up of ten tribes. Jeroboam, Solomon's servant, became king. Rehoboam was left with the tribe of Judah and later Benjamin was added. The reason for the division was because of Solomon's lust for foreign women who divided his heart so that he worshiped their false gods. Solomon had a divided heart, so God divided his Kingdom. It is ironic that both Israel and Judah had 20 kings before they both were carried off into captivity. Most of the kings of both kingdoms were considered evil according to God's standards. There were some that pleased God, but not many.

God sent prophets to testify against both nations to turn from their evil ways and to keep God's commandments, but they would not hear. They stiffened their necks and rejected His statutes and His covenant that He had made with their fathers. A long list of sins of both kingdoms are listed in 2 Kings 17:6-18 but they include the worship of false gods and the sacrificing of their children. The main reason the Israelites failed God was that they lost sight of Him.

> *"Where there is no vision (of God) the people cast off restraints."*
>
> *Proverbs 29:18*

The kings should have learned from the mistakes of their forefathers and listened to the prophets that God sent in order to avoid severe discipline. The failure to honor the revealed will of God results in ruin and destruction. The northern kingdom, Israel, was the first to fall in 722 BC. God used Assyria to carry away the ten tribes of the northern kingdom to discipline them for their sins.

Judah, the southern kingdom, also did not follow the Lord, but acted much like the northern kingdom, Israel. They worshipped false gods from the nations around them and they sacrificed their children by burning them alive. But Judah disobeyed God in another way that in our culture today would seem very odd. When Moses received the law from the Lord on Mount Sinai, He commanded His people:

> *Speak to the children of Israel and say to them: 'When you come into the land which I give you, then the land shall keep a sabbath to the Lord. Six years you shall sow your field, and six years you shall prune your vineyard, and gather its fruit; but in the seventh year there shall be a sabbath of solemn rest for the land, a sabbath to the Lord. You shall neither sow your field nor prune your vineyard. What grows of its own accord of your harvest you shall not reap, nor gather the grapes of your untended vine for it is a year of rest for the land.*
>
> *Leviticus 25:1-5*

The people of Israel were God's chosen people (and still are). In this sense, God owns the people and He owns the land that he "gave" to them. He has the right to tell the people what to do. But it is not out of anger or spite that He gives commandments to the people He loves. All of God's commandments are for the good of the people. When the people obey, God blesses them.

When God gave the Israelites the command to rest the land every seventh year, it was for their good. One year in seven they were to "leave fallow" the land to restore it to full productivity and so that the people who farmed it could rest. God promised that year six of the seven-year rotation, the land would produce double, so that the people could eat from the production of the sixth year while the land rested on the seventh (Leviticus 25:20-21).

Evidently the people did not trust that God would give them enough on the sixth year and so they did not rest the land on the seventh. This showed that they did not trust that God would be faithful to them. They lacked the faith in God that he would do what He promised. Is this any different than not believing God when He promises that His people will have enough when they tithe? (Malachi 3:8-10)

To some, this sounds like a minor violation to God's law, but to God this was not a minor violation. Because of this sin and others already mentioned, God sent the Babylonians to take Judah captive. Jeremiah, the prophet, prophesied that this would come to pass. He told the people:

> *"And the Lord has sent to you all His servants the prophets, rising early and sending them, but you have not listened nor inclined your ear to hear. They said, 'Repent now everyone of his evil way and his evil doings, and dwell in the land that the Lord has given to you and your fathers forever and ever. Do not go after other gods to serve them and worship them, and do not provoke Me to anger with the works of your hands; and I will not harm you.'*

*"Yet you have not listened to Me," says the Lord, "that you might provoke Me to anger with the works of your hands to your own hurt. Therefore thus says the Lord of hosts: 'Because you have not heard My words, behold, I will send and take all the families of the north,' says the Lord, 'and Nebuchadnezzar the king of Babylon, **My servant**, and will bring them against this land against its inhabitants, and against these nations all around, and will utterly destroy them, and make them an astonishment, a hissing, and perpetual desolations. Moreover, I will take from them the voice of mirth and the voice of gladness, the voice of the bridegroom and the voice of the bride, the sound of the millstones and the light of the lamp. And this whole land shall be a desolation and an astonishment, and these nations shall serve the king of Babylon **seventy years**.*

Jeremiah 25:4-11.

The seventy years of captivity was not a number picked out of someone's hat. That was the exact number of years that the Israelites had not given the land its Sabbath rest.

As long as she (the land) lay desolate she kept Sabbath, to fulfill seventy years.

2 Chronicles 36:21b

The deportation of the Israelites to Babylon happened in three stages. The first was in 605 BC when Nebuchadnezzar invaded Judah and took back Daniel, Shadrack, Meshack and Abednego to Babylon as well as some of the vessels from the temple. 597 BC saw Ezekiel and others deported with the rest of the national treasurers. The Babylonians took King Zedekiah in 588 BC and they laid a siege on Jerusalem for 18 months. Then Jerusalem fell in 568 BC. The temple was burned, and the walls were destroyed.

Daniel arrived in Babylon as a teenager in 605 BC and became a public servant until Cyrus, the Persian, became King.

PROPHECIES MADE	PROPHECIES FULFILLED
JEREMIAH 25:4-11 Jeremiah prophesied that Nebuchadnezzar of Babylon would burn the Temple, destroy the walls and take the people captive.	2 KINGS 25:1-11 Nebuchadnezzar did exactly as Jeremiah had prophesied.

QUESTIONS FOR DISCUSSION

Do you believe that the warning God sent to the Jewish people in Deuteronomy 11:26-28 should be sent to us as a nation?

In Jeremiah 25:9 God through the mouth of Jeremiah referred to Nebuchadnezzar, king of Babylon, as "His servant." Does that seem strange to you that God would use the Jews' enemy to discipline them? Could He do the same to the USA?

CHAPTER 10: NEBUCHADNEZZAR'S DREAM

The year 586 BC marked the beginning of the Israelites' 70-year captivity in Babylon. That was the year that the final wave of people from Judah were taken to Babylon. Solomon's Temple was burned, and the city walls of Jerusalem were torn down.

Daniel was taken to Babylon along with other outstanding young Jewish boys. This happened in the year 605 BC, the first year of the reign of Nebuchadnezzar. A year later, the Babylonian King had a dream. He wanted his wise men to not only tell him what the dream meant, but also what the dream was. Of course, none of them could do it. This made the king furious and he ordered his wise men killed. Daniel and his companions were also on that list. Daniel asked his friends to pray for him. He went to the king and requested some time so that he could interpret the dream. In a night vision, God told Daniel what the dream was and what it meant.

Daniel went to King Nebuchadnezzar and told him his dream:

> *"You O king, were watching; and behold, a great image! This great image, whose splendor was excellent, stood before you; and its form was awesome. This image's head was of fine gold, its chest and arms of silver, its*

belly and thighs of bronze, its legs of iron, its feet partly of iron and partly of clay. You watched while a stone was cut out without hands, which struck the image on its feet of iron and clay and broke them in pieces. Then the iron, the clay, the bronze, the silver, and the gold were crushed together, and became like chaff from the summer threshing floors; the wind carried them away so that no trace of them was found. And the stone that struck the image became a great mountain and filled the whole earth."

Daniel 2:31-35.

Daniel, after telling King Nebuchadnezzar's dream, immediately told him the interpretation of it:

"You, O king, are a king of kings. For the God of heaven has given you a kingdom, power, strength, and glory; and wherever the children of men dwell, or the beasts of the field and the birds of the heaven, He has given them into your hand, and has made you ruler over them all-you are this head of gold. But after you shall arise another kingdom inferior to yours; then another, a third kingdom of bronze, which shall rule over all the earth. And the fourth kingdom shall be as strong as iron, inasmuch as iron breaks in pieces and shatters everything; and like iron that crushes, that kingdom will break in pieces and crush all the

others. Whereas you saw the feet and toes, partly of potter's clay and partly of iron, the kingdom shall be divided; yet the strength of the iron shall be in it, just as you saw the iron mixed with ceramic clay. And as the toes of the feet were partly of iron and partly of clay, so the kingdom shall be partly strong and partly fragile. As you saw iron mixed with ceramic clay, they will mingle with the seed of men; but they will not adhere to one another, just as iron does not mix with clay. And in the days of these kings the God of heaven will set up a kingdom which shall never be destroyed; and the kingdom shall not be left to other people; it shall break in pieces and consume all these kingdoms, and it shall stand forever. Inasmuch as you saw that the stone was cut out of the mountain without hands, and that it broke in pieces the iron, the bronze, the clay, the silver, and the gold-the great God has made known to the king what will come to pass after this. The dream is certain, and its interpretation is sure."

Daniel 2:37-45.

Nebuchadnezzar's dream as interpreted by Daniel covers a vast amount of time. Daniel was written in the 6th century BC. The prophecy within it covers from that time and its end is yet to come. A statue representing the four kingdoms was made up of four different medals-gold, silver, bronze and iron. The king dreamed about his own kingdom-the Babylonian Kingdom represented by the "head of **gold**." Nebuchadnezzar was the supreme authority in the world of his day. His empire was not as large as the later kingdoms, nor did it last as long, but he exercised absolute control as no one after him did.

The chest and arms of **silver** represented the joint kingdom of Media and Persia. Together they defeated Babylon in the year of 539 BC. That empire lasted until 331 BC or 208 years. The two arms of silver represent the two nations, less powerful, but covered a bigger area

The third kingdom-the abdomen and thighs of **bronze** was Greece. It lasted 300 years from 331 BC until 31 BC, longer than Babylonia or the Media-Persia empires. Alexander the Great died in 323 BC and his kingdom was divided up by his four generals. The empire was more democratic which gave more power to the people and less to its rulers. The two bronze thighs of the statue represented the two major divisions of the Greek Empire: its eastern (Syria) and western (Egypt) sectors.

Rome defeated the Greek Empire in 31 BC and was represented by the lower part of the legs of the statue which was made of iron. The Western Roman Empire lasted until 476 AD and the Eastern until 1453 AD. Both crushed all opposition with a brutal strength that surpassed any of its predecessors, but, in terms of absolute authority, Rome was the least powerful of the four empires. Just as each succeeding metal was less valuable than the one before it, each succeeding empire was less powerful internally than its predecessors.

No outside power ever defeated the Roman Empire. It fell apart from within-no enemy destroyed it. In that sense, it still exists. Rome is living in the nations of Europe today: Italy, France, Great Britain, Germany, and Spain are all part of the old Roman Empire. Could it be that the ten toes of iron with clay between is a representation of the modern European Union? Individually they may be strong, but the clay that holds them together is weak. Brexit is an example of the weakness of the EU to hold its members together. A problem with this theory is that there are more than ten countries currently in the EU. But if this is the correct interpretation of the ten toes, God can get it reduced to that number!

The stone that was cut out without hands is the force that will strike the ten toes and break them into pieces. Then the empires of iron, bronze, silver and gold will be crushed together, and they will become like chaff and be blown away. The stone will become a mountain and fill the earth.

We have established that the four great empires of the earth were represented by the statue made up of four different medals. It is Jesus Christ at His second coming that is that stone which will destroy the kingdoms of this world and will rule in his Kingdom worldwide forever.

PROPHECIES MADE	PROPHECIES FULFILLED
Daniel 2:31-40 Daniel's vision of 4 empires that would rule the world	Biblical Accounts, Secular History Babylon, Media Persia, Greece & Rome all came into power
Daniel 2:41-45 Stone cut from mountain without hands (Christ) will destroy all earthly kingdoms and He will rule Heaven and earth forever.	Yet to be fulfilled Will be fulfilled at His 2nd coming. Earthly kingdoms will be no more and He will reign forever.

Since we know that the first part of Daniel's prophecy has been fulfilled, what are the odds that the second will be also?

Sometimes we underestimate the power of prayer when we ask others to pray/fast for us in difficult situations. Daniel 2:17-18, Mark 14:38 and Esther 4:16 are verses that illustrate individuals asking others to pray. Who were they? Why did they ask for prayer? Why do we sometimes hesitate to ask others to pray for us?

CHAPTER 11: RULE OF THE MEDES AND PERSIANS

The year was 539 BC and Belshazzar was king of Babylon. Belshazzar, son of Nebuchadnezzar, (actually grandson) decided to throw a huge party (Daniel 5). Even though his enemy, the Medes and Persians had surrounded the city of Babylon, Belshazzar felt secure because Babylon had not fallen to an invading army for 1,000 years. The city was surrounded by a moat and a wall 76 feet in width with a height of 304. The River Euphrates divided the city. It ran swift and deep.

With the armies of a conqueror pressing at the city, Belshazzar took refuge in an orgy of wine with all his lords, wives and concubines. They drank from gold vessels that had been taken by King Nebuchadnezzar when the Temple in Jerusalem was destroyed years ago. This was an act of open defiance to insult the God whose Temple had stood in Jerusalem. The night of revelry became a night of revelation when the fingers of a man's hand appeared and wrote on the wall in front of the King. Some speculate that in all history, this was the fastest anyone had ever sobered up. The Bible records that "the king's countenance changed, and his thoughts troubled him, so that the joints of his hips were loosened, and his knees knocked against each other." (Daniel 5:6) The king's "wise men" could neither read nor interpret the meaning of the writing.

Daniel, who was in his 80's by now, was brought before the king and promised gifts if he could tell the king the meaning of the writing on the wall. Daniel reviewed all that God had done to humble his grandfather Nebuchadnezzar. Daniel told Belshazzar that he knew all about his grandfather's experiences, but his heart was full of pride, evidenced by the sacrilegious use of the Temple vessels.

The words on the wall

מנא מנא תקל ופרסין

("MENE, MENE, TEKEL, UPHARSIN") were interpreted by Daniel. Their meaning was, "God has numbered your kingdom, and finished it. You have been weighed in the balances and found wanting; Your kingdom has been divided and given to the Medes and Persians." (Daniel 5:26-28) Verses 30 and 31 say "that very night (October 13, 539 BC) Belshazzar, king of the Chaldeans, was slain. And Darius the Mede received the kingdom…" This was all prophesied in much detail in Jeremiah 51:33-58 and in Isaiah 13:17-22:

> *"Behold, I will stir up the Medes against them, who will not regard silver; and as for gold, they will not delight in it. Also, their bows will dash the young men to pieces, and they will have no pity on the fruit of the womb; their eye will not spare children. And Babylon, the glory of kingdoms, the beauty of the Chaldeans' pride,*

How the Medes and Persians took over the "impenetrable" city of Babylon is not recorded in the Bible, but there are many reliable documents that describe what took place. The Persians diverted the water from the Euphrates River that flowed south through Babylon into an ancient lake located to the north. This allowed them to walk into the city on the riverbed and scale the undefended walls that flanked the river.

Thus, the "head of gold" was replaced by the "chest and arms of silver", prophesied in Nebuchadnezzar's dream in Daniel 2:31-35. The Media-Persian Empire policies concerning captured peoples was opposite that of the Babylonians. The Babylonians believed that it was best to keep their captives long term to prevent rebellion in the future. The Media-Persians on the other hand practiced letting defeated people return to their homeland which would please them and would discourage them from rebelling.

By bringing an end to the Babylonian Empire and bringing in a nation who had a more lenient policy toward captive people, God was setting up a scenario that would get a remnant of the Jews back to Judea. But first they must repent of their sins and those of their fathers that brought on the captivity in the first place. Moses, inspired by the Holy Spirit, wrote this promise in Leviticus:

> *"But if they confess their iniquity and the iniquity of their fathers, with their unfaithfulness in which they were unfaithful to Me, and that they also have walked contrary to Me, and that I also have walked contrary to them and have brought them into the land of their enemies; if their uncircumcised hearts are humbled, and they accept their guilt-then I will remember My covenant with Jacob, and My covenant with Isaac and My covenant with Abraham I will remember; **I will remember the land.** The land also shall be left empty by them and **will enjoy its sabbaths while it lies desolate without them**; they will accept their guilt, because they despised My judgments and because their soul abhorred My statutes. Yet for all that, when they are in the land of their enemies, I will not cast them away, nor shall I abhor them, to utterly destroy them and break My covenant with them; for I am the*

Lord their God. But for their sake I will remember the covenant of their ancestors, whom I brought out of the land of Egypt in the sight of the nations, that I might be their God: I am the Lord."

Leviticus 26:40-45

God can use any means to fulfill the Abrahamic Covenant to his people-even a gentile King. Proverbs 21:1 says, ***"The king's heart is in the hand of the Lord, Like the rivers of water; He turns it wherever He wishes."*** The first year that Cyrus (Daniel 9:1 calls him "Darius" which may have been a title) became King. Daniel:

*"understood by the books the number of the years specified by the word of the Lord through Jeremiah the prophet, that He would accomplish **seventy years** in the desolations of Jerusalem."*

Daniel 9:2

The passage that Daniel was reading was from Jeremiah:

"For thus says the Lord: After seventy years are completed at Babylon, I will visit you and perform My good word toward you and cause you to return to this place. For I know the thoughts that I think toward you, says the Lord,

thoughts of peace and not of evil, to give you a future and a hope."

Jeremiah 29:10-11

Daniel undoubtedly had read the passage from Leviticus admonishing the people to repent so that God would permit His people to return to their promised land. Daniel 9:3-19 records his heartfelt prayer of repentance for himself, his people and their forefathers. (O that America would gather as one and pray that prayer!)

In the first year of Cyrus, (537 BC) the **gentile** king of Media-Persia, made this proclamation:

"Now in the first year of Cyrus king of Persia, that the word of the Lord by the mouth of Jeremiah might be fulfilled, the Lord stirred up the spirit of Cyrus king of Persia, so that he made a proclamation throughout all his kingdom, and also put it in writing, saying, 'Thus says Cyrus king of Persia: All the kingdoms of the earth the Lord God of heaven has given me. And He has commanded me to build Him a house at Jerusalem which is in Judah. Who is among you of all His people? May his God be with him, and let him go up to Jerusalem, which is in Judah, and build the house of the Lord God of Israel (He is God), which is in Jerusalem. And whoever is left in any place where he dwells, let the men of his

place help him with silver and gold, with goods and livestock, besides the freewill offerings for the house of God which is in Jerusalem.

Ezra 1:1-4

With this proclamation began the return of the Israelites to their country. The number of this first wave of returning people was 49,897 (Ezra 2:64). These people represented all twelve tribes of Israel, not just the tribes of Judah and Benjamin. (Ezra 6:17 and Acts 26:7)

PROPHECIES MADE	PROPHECIES FULFILLED
Isaiah 13:17-22 Prophecy of the fall of Babylon by the Medes and Persians	Daniel 5 King Belshazzar lost his kingdom to the Medes and Persians
Jeremiah 29:10-11 After 70 years of captivity in Babylon, God would cause the Israelites to return to Jerusalem in Judea	Ezra 1:1-4 God commanded King Cyrus of Persia to build Him a house in Judah, thus releasing the Israelites to go back home to build it

QUESTIONS FOR DISCUSSION

It was Belshazzar's pride that caused him to lose the kingdom. Looking back in history, have we ever seen the pride of a ruler cause him to be replaced by another? Why is it that God says he hates pride? (Proverbs 6:16-19) What is the fall of a nation or individual usually preceded by? (Proverbs 16:18)

Babylon trusted in their walls to keep them safe which proved to be a mistake. What are some things that we trust in to keep us safe? Who is the only One who can ultimately keep us safe?

Cyrus was a gentile king that God used to bless the Jewish people. What other gentiles has God used to bless Israelites?

CHAPTER 12: REBUILDING THE TEMPLE AND WALLS OF JERUSALEM

King Cyrus' decree in 537 BC sent almost 50,000 captives back to Jerusalem to rebuild the Temple. Zerubbabel would be the person in charge of building the Temple, but his uncle, Sheshbazar, was the one chosen to lead the people back to Jerusalem. Zerubbabel was the grandson of King Jehoiachin who was taken into captivity by Nebuchadnezzar.

The foundation of the Temple was laid, but then the building stopped because of opposition from Israel's enemies. In 520 BC Darius II confirmed Cyrus' proclamation and the building restarted and was finished five years later in 515 BC.

There are two ways in which the 70-year captivity prophecy was fulfilled. Using the first deportation from Judah as the beginning (605 BC) to the beginning of the Temple Reconstruction (536 BC) is the first. The second was when the last wave of captives went to Babylon and the first Temple was destroyed (586 BC) to when the second Temple was completed (515 BC). I used the second (586 BC to 515 BC) in my timeline but either or both could be correct.

To mark the completion of the Temple:

Seventy years after the second Temple was completed, Nehemiah, a Jewish man and cupbearer to the Persian King Artaxerxes, got word that the walls and gates of Jerusalem were destroyed. Nehemiah was one of the captives taken to Babylon by Nebuchadnezzar, but his parents were buried in Jerusalem. This news grieved Nehemiah greatly. He, like Daniel, prayed for forgiveness for the sins of Israel (Nehemiah 1:5-11 and Daniel 9:3-19).

In his prayer, Nehemiah reminded God the words that He spoke to Moses (the Mosaic Covenant):

Nehemiah 1:8-9.

Nehemiah, like Daniel, must have known that God was not done sending His people back to Jerusalem. Although the Temple had been built, the city was in shambles. The walls and the infrastructure of the city needed to be rebuilt.

While attending to his duties as cupbearer for the King, King Artaxerxes noticed that Nehemiah was incredibly sad. When asked why he was so sorrowful, Nehemiah told him about the conditions of his home-Jerusalem. The King asked him what his request would be. Nehemiah prayed "to the God of Heaven" and replied that he would like to go to Jerusalem to repair the walls there. So, on March 14, 445 BC, it pleased the king to send Nehemiah to Jerusalem to repair the walls. Despite opposition from their enemies, Nehemiah and the families of the Israelites finished the walls in 52 days!

That date, March 14, 445 BC, is one of the most important dates on God's prophetic calendar. It is the beginning date of the 70 Weeks of Years as prophesied in Daniel 9. Daniel wrote in that chapter that the Jewish captivity would last 70 years as recorded in Jeremiah. As he was praying for the forgiveness of the sins of his people, the angel

Gabriel appeared to him. Gabriel told him that he was greatly loved, and he had come to give him skill to understand. He said:

> *"Seventy weeks (of years or 490 years) are determined for your people (the Jewish People) and for your Holy City (Jerusalem),* **to finish the transgression** *(end rebellion against God),* **to make an end of sins** *(it will end human failure to obey God),* **to make reconciliation for iniquity** *(it will provide time for atonement that will cover human wickedness),* **to bring in everlasting righteousness** *(it will inaugurate a new society in which righteousness prevails),* **to seal up vision and prophecy** *(it will bring in the fulfillment of the vision that God has for the earth),* **and to anoint the Most Holy** *(a reference to the third Temple). Know therefore and understand, that* **from the going forth of the command to restore and build Jerusalem** *(Artaxerxes command to Nehemiah on March 14, 445 BC)* **until Messiah the Prince** *(Jesus entered Jerusalem April 6, 32 AD), there shall be seven weeks and sixty-two weeks; the street shall be built again, and the wall, even in troublesome times.* **And after sixty-two weeks Messiah shall be cut off** *(crucified by the Romans), but not for Himself;* **and the people of the prince** *(Roman General Titus in*

The "seventy week (of years) or 490 years is divided up into three periods of time. The first is the 7 weeks or 49 years. This was probably the time needed to not only build the walls (which was completed in 52 days) but also to build the infrastructure of the city and remove debris. Then, secondly, there is the 62 weeks or 434 years that covers the time after the rebuilding of the city until Jesus entered the city April 6, 32 AD. The combination of the 7 weeks and the 62 weeks equals 483 years or using the lunar calendar (which was used at that time) 173,880 days (483 x 360 days). 173,880 is the exact number of days between March 14, 445 BC when Artaxerxes gave the command to Nehemiah to the day that Jesus entered the city on a donkey and was "cut off" (crucified) just a few days later.

some of the Pharisees called to Him from the crowd, 'teacher, rebuke Your disciples.' But He answered and said to them, 'I tell you that if these should keep silent, the stones would immediately cry out.' Now as He drew near, He saw the city and wept over it, saying, 'If you had known, even you, especially in this your day, the things that make for our peace! But now they are hidden from your eyes. For days will come upon you when your enemies will build an embankment around you, surround you and close you in on every side, and level you, and your children within you, to the ground; and they will not leave in you one stone upon another because you did not know the time of your visitation.'"

Luke 19:37-44

One might wonder why Jesus was so distressed as He entered Jerusalem that April morning. After all the crowds were praising Him and seemed to recognize Him for who He is. Some in the crowd were his disciples who the Pharisees wanted to silence, but there were others in the city including the Pharisees that wanted Him dead. As a whole, the Jewish people had rejected Him as their spiritual Savior. They wanted a leader who could get them out from under the Roman rule. When it became obvious to them that Jesus was not the man for that, they rejected Him.

Jesus recognized and always knew that He would be rejected by the Jews, but as He looked down on the city from the Mount of Olives, the thought of their rejection caused Him to weep (the Greek word is Wail). This was not a quiet cry, it was a loud, severe mourning that came from deep in His gut. He also knew what the consequences of that rejection would be. He knew that thirty-eight years later, Titus, the Roman General would destroy the Temple, the city and its people including the children and it broke His heart.

It did not have to be that way. The religious leaders had the words of Daniel and if they would have done the math, they would have known that 173,880 days after March 14, 445 BC when Artaxerxes sent Nehemiah to Jerusalem to rebuild its walls that Jesus, their King, would arrive in their city. They could have had His peace, but they rejected it.

Going back to the information that Gabriel gave Daniel, there were six events that would come to pass during those 70 weeks of years (490 years). The crucifixion of Jesus was the end of 69 weeks. Only one of the six prophecies has been fulfilled, that being "making reconciliation for iniquity." Jesus fulfilled that when he took the sins of the whole world upon Himself, died and rose again so that all who trust Him to have their sins forgiven would have eternal life. The other five; "to finish the transgressions" (when people quit rebelling against God), "to make an end of sin" (when people quit disobeying God), "to bring in everlasting righteousness" (when God brings in a new society where righteous prevails), "to seal up visions and prophecy (all prophecy will be fulfilled) and "to anoint the Most Holy" (the third Temple will be built in Jerusalem) have not happened yet.

Only one of the weeks (of years) is left. That seven-year period will begin after the Rapture of the Church when the Church will meet Jesus in the "air," and He will then take them to Heaven. (1 Thessalonians 4:16-17) The 70th week will be reserved for God's punishment (the Tribulation) upon the earth and then Christ will return, and His Millennial Reign on earth will begin. Most conservative scholars believe that the other five prophesies given to Daniel will happen after the Rapture. More information about the Rapture and the 70th week will be covered later in this study.

PROPHECIES MADE	PROPHECIES FULFILLED
Daniel 9:24 Jesus will make reconciliation for iniquity	Romans 4:25 Jesus was crucified for our offenses and raised for our justification.
Daniel 9:26 After 62 "weeks" the Messiah shall be cut off	Luke 23:33 At Calvary, they crucified Him
Daniel 9:26 The Prince (Titus) will destroy the Temple and walls.	70 AD As prophesied, Roman General, Titus destroyed the Temple and walls of Jerusalem.

QUESTIONS FOR DISCUSSION

In 70 AD, Titus the Roman general destroyed the city of Jerusalem and its Temple. Jesus said twice in Luke 19:44 and Mark 13:2 that not one stone of the temple would be left on another. Why would the Romans go to that much trouble to remove those huge stones from on top of each other?

CHAPTER 13: FULFILLED AND UNFULFILLED PROPHECIES ABOUT JESUS

Prophecies about Jesus' birth, life, death and resurrection are found in many books of the Old Testament. For any one man outside of Jesus to fulfill these prophecies would be impossible to say the least. The following Old Testament prophecies followed by their verses of fulfillment are in chronological order. By reading and meditating on these scriptures, may the Holy Spirit touch your heart as you read about the God-Man that came to earth to teach us how to live and overcome death so that we may also live with Him forever.

Jesus is to be born of a virgin and His name called Immanuel (God with us).

> *"Therefore, the Lord Himself will give you a sign: Behold, the **virgin** shall conceive and bear a Son, and shall call His name Immanuel."*

> *Isaiah 7:14*

> *"Now the birth of Jesus Christ was as follows: After His mother Mary was betrothed to Joseph, **before they came together,** she was found with Child of the Holy Spirit.*

Jesus is to be born in Bethlehem.

*"But you, **Bethlehem** Ephrathah, though you are little among the thousands of Judah, yet out of you shall come forth to Me the one to be Ruler in Israel, whose goings forth are from of old, from everlasting.*

Micah 5:2

*"Joseph also went up from Galilee, out of the city of Nazareth, into Judea to the city of David, which is called **Bethlehem**, because he was of the house and lineage of David, to be registered with Mary, his betrothed wife, who was with child. So it was that while they were there, the days were completed for her to be delivered. And she brought forth her first-born Son, and wrapped Him in swaddling cloths, and laid Him in a manger, because there was no room for them in the inn."*

Luke 2:4-6

The wise men to be guided by a star.

*"I see Him, but not now; I behold Him, but not near; A **Star** shall come out of Jacob; A Scepter shall rise out of Israel…"*

Numbers 24:17

*"Now after Jesus was born in Bethlehem of Judea in the days of Herod the king, behold, wise men from the East came to Jerusalem, saying, 'Where is He who has been born King of the Jews? For we have seen His **Star** in the East and have come to worship Him.'"*

Matthew 2:1-2

The wise men bring gifts to Jesus.

*"The multitude of camels shall cover your land, the dromedaries of Median and Ephah; all those from Sheba shall come; They shall bring **gold and incense**, and they shall proclaim the praises of the Lord.*

Isaiah 60:6

*"And when they had come into the house, they saw the young Child with Mary His mother, and fell down and worshiped Him. And when they had opened their treasures, they presented gifts to Him: **gold, frankincense, and myrrh**.*

Matthew 2:11

Mary and Joseph take Jesus to Egypt to flee from Herod.

*"When Israel was a Child, I loved Him, and out of **Egypt** I called My Son.*

Hosea 11:1

*"When he arose, he took the young Child and His mother by night and departed for Egypt, and was there until the death of Herod, that it might be fulfilled which was spoken by the Lord through the prophet, saying, 'Out of **Egypt** I called My Son.'"*

Matthew 2:14-15

Herod kills the baby boys in Bethlehem.

*"A voice was heard in Ramah, lamentation and bitter weeping, Rachel weeping for her children, refusing to be comforted for her children because **they are no more**.*

Jeremiah 31:15

*"When Herod, when he saw that he was deceived by the wise men, was exceedingly angry; and he sent forth and **put to death all the male children who were in Bethlehem** and in all its districts, from two years old and under, according to the time which he had determined from the wise men."*

Matthew 2:16

John announces the coming of Jesus.

*"The voice of **one crying in the wilderness**: 'Prepare the way of the Lord; Make straight in the desert a highway for our God.*

Isaiah 40:3

*"In those days **John the Baptist came preaching in the wilderness** of Judea, and saying, 'Repent, for the kingdom of heaven is at hand!' For this is He who was spoken of by the prophet Isaiah, saying: 'The voice of one crying in the wilderness: 'Prepare the way of the Lord; make His paths straight.'"*

Matthew 3:1-3

The Holy Spirit descends upon Jesus at His Baptism.

*"There shall come forth a Rod from the stem of Jesse, and a Branch shall grow out of his roots. **The Spirit of the Lord shall rest upon Him**, the spirit of wisdom and understanding, the Spirit of counsel and might, the Spirit of knowledge and of the fear of the Lord."*

Isaiah 11:1-2

*"When He had been baptized, Jesus came up immediately from the water; and behold, the heavens were opened to Him, and **He saw the Spirit of God descending like a dove and alighting upon Him**. And suddenly a voice*

came from heaven saying, 'This is My beloved Son, in whom I am well pleased.'"

Matthew 3:16-17

Jesus heals the blind, the deaf, the lame and the dumb shall sing.

*"Then **the eyes of the blind shall be opened, and the ears of the deaf shall be unstopped**. Then the lame shall leap like a deer, and **the tongue of the dumb sing.***

Isaiah 35:5-6a

*"The Spirit of the Lord God is upon Me, because the Lord has anointed Me to **preach good tidings to the poor;** He has sent Me to heal the brokenhearted to proclaim liberty to the captives and the opening of the prison to those who are bound; to proclaim the acceptable year of the Lord.*

Isaiah 61:1-2a

*Jesus answered and said to them, "Go and tell John the things which you hear and see: The **blind see** and **the lame walk;** the lepers are cleansed and the **deaf hear;** the dead are raised up and the **poor have the gospel preached to them."***

Matthew 11:4-5

Jesus rides into Jerusalem on a donkey.

*"Rejoice greatly, O daughter of Zion! Shout, O daughter of Jerusalem! Behold, your King is coming to you: He is just and having salvation, lowly and **riding on a donkey,** a colt, the foal of a donkey.*

Zechariah 9:9

*"They brought the **donkey** and the colt, laid their clothes on them and set Him on them. And a very great multitude spread their clothes on the road; others cut down branches from the trees and spread them on the road. Then the multitudes who went before and those who followed cried out saying: 'Hosanna to the Son of David! Blessed is He who comes in the name of the Lord! Hosanna in the highest!"*

Matthew 21:7-9

Jesus is betrayed for 30 pieces of silver.

*"Then I said to them, 'If it is agreeable to you, give me my wages; and if not, refrain,' So they weighed out for my wages **thirty pieces of silver**.*

Zechariah 11:12

*"Then one of the twelve, called Judas Iscariot, went to the chief priests and said, 'What are you willing to give me if I deliver Him to You?" And they counted out to him **thirty pieces of silver.***

Matthew 26:14-15

Judas throws the 30 pieces into the House of the Lord, the price for the Potters Field.

*"And the Lord said to me, 'Throw it to the potter'-that princely price they set on me. So, I took the thirty pieces of silver and threw them into the house of the Lord for the **potter**.*

Zechariah 11:13

*"Then he (Judas) threw down the pieces of silver in the temple and departed and went and hanged himself. But the chief priests took the silver pieces and said, 'It is not lawful to put them into the treasury, because they are the price of blood.' And they consulted together and bought with them the **potter's field,** to bury strangers in. Therefore, that field has been called the Field of Blood to this day.*

Matthew 27:5-8

All His disciples desert Jesus.

*"Awake, O sword, against My Shepherd,
against the Man who is My Companion," says
the Lord of hosts, "Strike the Shepherd, and*
the sheep will be scattered*…."*

Zechariah 13:7a

*In that hour Jesus said to the multitudes,
"Have you come out, as against a robber, with
swords and clubs to take Me? I sat daily with
you, teaching in the temple, and you did not
seize Me. But all this was done that the
Scriptures of the prophets might be fulfilled."*
Then all the disciples forsook Him and fled.

Matthew 26:55-56

Jesus is silent before His accusers.

*"He was oppressed, and He was afflicted, yet
He opened not His mouth; He was led as a
lamb to the slaughter, and as a sheep before
its shearers is silent,* ***so He opened not his
mouth****.*

Isaiah 53:7

*"And while He was being accused by the chief
priests and elders,* ***He answered nothing****.
Then Pilate said to Him, 'Do you not hear how
many things they testify against You?' But He
answered him not one word, so that the
governor marveled greatly.*

Matthew 27:12-14

Jesus is scourged and ridiculed.

*"**I gave My back to those who struck Me**,
and My cheeks to those who plucked out the
beard; **I did not hide My face from shame
and spitting**."*

Isaiah 50:6

*"Then **they spat in His face and beat Him**;
and others **struck Him with the palms** of their
hands, saying, 'Prophesy to us, Christ! Who is
the one who struck You?'"*

Matthew 26:67-68

*"Then he released Barabbas to them; and
when he had **scourged Jesus**, he delivered
Him to be crucified.*

Matthew 27:26

The soldiers gamble for His clothes.

*"They divide My garments among them, and
for My clothing they cast lots."*

Psalms 22:18

*"Then the soldiers, when they had crucified
Jesus, took His garments and made four parts,
to each soldier a part, and also the tunic. Now*

*the tunic was without seam, woven from the top in one piece. They said therefore among themselves, 'Let us not tear it, **but cast lots for it**, whose it shall be,' that the Scripture might be fulfilled…"*

John 19:23-24

The chief priests and others mock Him on the cross.

*"All those who see **Me ridicule Me**; they shoot out the lip, they shake the head, saying, He trusted in the Lord**, let Him rescue Him**; let Him deliver Him,, since He delights in Him!"*

Psalms 22:7-8

*And those who passed by **blasphemed Him,** wagging their heads and saying, "You who destroy the temple and build it in three days, save Yourself! If you are the Son of God, come down from the cross." Likewise, the chief priests also mocking with the scribes and elders, said," He saved others; Himself He can not save. If He is the King of Israel, let Him now come down from the cross, and we will believe Him. **He trusted in God; let Him deliver Him** now if He will have Him; for He said, 'I am the Son of God.'"*

Matthew 27:39-43

Jesus cries out in His isolation from His Father.

> ***"My God, My God, why have You forsaken Me?*** *Why are You so far from helping Me?"*

> *Psalms 22:1*

> *Now when the sixth hour had come, there was darkness over the whole land until the ninth hour. And at the ninth hour Jesus cried out with a loud voice, saying, "Eloi, Eloi, lama sabachthani?" which is translated,* ***"My God, My God, why have You forsaken Me?***

> *Mark 15:33-34*

Jesus suffers a terrible thirst.

> *"My strength is dried up like a potsherd, and* ***My tongue clings to My jaws****; You have brought Me to the dust of death.*

> *Psalms 22:15*

> *After this, Jesus, knowing that all things were now accomplished, that the Scripture might be fulfilled, said,* ***"I thirst!"***

> *John 19:28*

Jesus is laid in a rich man's tomb.

> ***"And they made His grave*** *with the wicked— But* ***with the rich*** *at His death because He*

had done no violence, nor was any deceit in His mouth.

Isaiah 53:9

*"Now when evening had come, there came a **rich man** from Arimathea, named Joseph, who himself had also become a disciple of Jesus. This man went to Pilate and asked for the body of Jesus. Then Pilate commanded the body to be given to him. When Joseph had taken the body, he wrapped it in a clean linen cloth, **and laid it in his new tomb** which he had hewn out of the rock; and he rolled a large stone against the door of the tomb, and departed.*

Matthew 27:57-60

Jesus was tortured for our sin.

*"But He was **wounded** for our transgressions, He was **bruised** for our iniquities; the **chastisement** for our peace was upon Him and by His stripes we are healed.*

Isaiah 53:5

*"…who (Jesus) was **delivered up** because of our offenses and was raised because of our justification.*

Romans 4:25

Jesus bore our sins that we might obtain His righteousness.

*"He shall see the labor of His soul and be satisfied. By His knowledge, My **righteous** Servant shall justify many, for **He shall bear their iniquities**.*

Isaiah 53:11

*"For He made Him who knew no sin **to be sin for us**, that we might become the **righteousness** of God in Him."*

2 Corinthians 5:21

Jesus will return to earth with power and great glory!

*"I was watching in the night visions, and behold, **One like the Son of Man, coming with the clouds of heaven!** He came to the Ancient of Days, and they brought Him near before Him. Then to Him was given dominion and glory and a kingdom, that all peoples, nations and languages should serve Him. His dominion is an everlasting dominion, which shall not pass away, and His kingdom the one which shall not be destroyed."*

Daniel 7:13-14

*"Then the sign of the **Son of Man will appear in heaven**, and then all the tribes of the earth will mourn, and they will see the Son of Man coming on the clouds of heaven with power and great glory."*

Matthew 24:30

Jesus will return to rule and reward those that love Him.

*"Behold, the Lord God shall come with a strong hand, and His arm shall rule for Him; Behold, **His reward is with Him** and his work is before Him.*

Isaiah 40:10

*"And behold, I am coming quickly, and **My reward is with Me**, to give to everyone according to his work."*

Revelation 22:12

Jesus is the Everlasting King of Heaven and Earth.

*"Who has performed and done it, calling the generations from the beginning? 'I, the Lord, am **the first; and with the last I AM He**.'"*

Isaiah 41:4

*"I AM the Alpha and the Omega, the Beginning and the End, the **First and the Last.**"*

Revelation 22:13

CHAPTER 14: PENTECOST AND REGATHERING OF GOD'S PEOPLE

Before Christ's death and resurrection, He promised that He would send a "Helper" after He left this earth.

> *"But the Helper, the Holy Spirit, whom the Father will send in My name, He will teach you all things, and bring to your remembrance all things that I said to you."*
>
> *John 14:26*

After His resurrection and before He ascended into Heaven, Jesus commanded his apostles to remain in Jerusalem. He reminded them of the promise of God sending them the Helper:

> *"…for John truly baptized with water, but you shall be baptized with the Holy Spirit not many days from now."*
>
> *Acts 1:5*

> *"But you shall receive power when the Holy Spirit has come upon you; and you shall be witnesses to Me in Jerusalem, and in all Judea and Samaria, and to the end of the earth."*
>
> *Acts 1:8*

On the day of Pentecost, God sent the Holy Spirit to those apostles and they began to speak in languages of others who were in Jerusalem from *"every nation under Heaven." (Acts 2:5)* And Peter, being filled with the Holy Spirit, testified about what Jesus had done and three thousand people were saved. The Gospel was no longer just for the Jews, but now gentiles were included, for Jesus commanded His apostles to be a witness for Him "to the end of the earth."

Pentecost was the first day of the Church Age that we are presently in. Thomas Constable, a former professor at Dallas Theological Seminary on page 11 in his notes on the book of Acts wrote:

> *After His ascension, Christ poured out His Holy Spirit on the day of Pentecost. This was the birthday of the church. The baptism of the Spirit did something God had never done before in history. It united believers with Christ in a new relationship: as fellow members of the spiritual body of Christ (John 14:17: "he abides with you and will be in you."). Believers then shared the life of Christ in a way never before experienced. God united them with Him. The same Spirit of God that indwelt Him now indwells us. The unity of the church is not external: what we believe (creeds), how we organize ourselves (polity), or where and how we meet (culture). It is internal" through Him who indwells us. The basis of our unity in the*

church goes back to the origin of the church. It began when the Holy Spirit first baptized believers on the day of Pentecost (1 Cor. 12:13; Rom. 8:9). The "church" is not just a new name for Israel.

After the 69 weeks of years and Christ's ascension into Heaven, God began to do something new. God had dealt mainly with the Jewish people since Abraham was promised the Land, Seed and Blessing. He temporarily is now working with the Gentiles and has blinded the eyes of the Jews. We are now in the Church Age, a period of time that Gentiles (non-Jews) can be saved in greater numbers than anytime previously. This is not to say that Jews cannot be saved in these days, but God has turned his emphasis toward the Gentiles. This is first, because of the Jews rejection of Jesus and secondly, God's desire that all people should be saved. Isaiah prophesied this:

> *"Make the heart of this people dull, and their ears heavy, and shut their eyes; lest they see with their eyes, and hear with their ears, and understand with their heart, and return and be healed."*
>
> *Isaiah 6:10*

The Apostle Paul was called by God to not only bring the Gospel to the Jews, but also to the Gentiles. Before his conversion on the road to Damascus,

Paul was a great persecutor of the Christians, but he became one of the greatest servants of Christ the world has ever seen. Speaking to Ananias, none other than Jesus Himself proclaimed the purpose of Paul's ministry:

> *"…He is a chosen vessel of Mine to bear My name before Gentiles, kings, and the children of Israel. For I will show him how many things he must suffer for My name's sake".*
>
> *Acts 9:15-16*

Paul is best known for his ministry to the Gentiles, but he would always preach first to the Jews. He did this because of his great love for the Jewish people (Read Romans 11) for he was a Jew also. On one of his missionary trips with Barnabas, his statement to the Jews at Antioch was recorded by Luke in Acts:

> *Then Paul and Barnabas grew bold and said, "It was necessary that the word of God should be spoken to you (the Jews) first; but since you reject it, and judge yourselves unworthy of everlasting life, behold, **we turn to the Gentiles.** For so the Lord has commanded us: 'I have set you as a light to the Gentiles, that you should be for salvation to the ends of the earth.'"*
>
> *Acts 13:46-47 (Paul quoted Isaiah 49:6)*

Even though God's emphasis is now focused on the Gentiles in this Church Age, He is not done with the Jews. After Jerusalem was destroyed by the Romans in 70 AD, the Jews were scattered across the world. The many prophecies in the Bible that the Jews would come back to their homeland in huge numbers were not believed by most people in the world. After all, no people after their country was destroyed and themselves scattered to the wind have ever come back to their original land to become a sovereign state and speak the same language! But nothing is too hard for God and He always keeps His promises! To Him be the Glory!

Since 70 AD life has been hard for the Jewish people. God brought them back to their land in 1948. But ever since then, many nations have tried to annihilate them and some still say they will. In Deuteronomy, Moses prophesied about the tough times they would face after 70 AD:

> *"Then the Lord will scatter you among all peoples, from one end of the earth to the other, and there you shall serve other gods, which neither you nor your fathers have known-wood and stone. And among those nations you will find no rest, nor shall the sole of your foot have a resting place; but there the Lord will give you a trembling heart, failing eyes, and anguish of soul. Your life shall hang in doubt before you; you shall fear day and night and have no assurance of life."*

For the last 2,000 years, bullies of the world have abused the Jews. One only has to think back to the 1940's and remember what Hitler's Third Reich did to God's people. Millions of Jews went to the gas chambers as Germany thought they had to have a "final solution" to the Jewish "problem." And now anti-Semitism is again rising in especially Europe and surprisingly in the United States. Somehow it has been forgotten that God "blesses those that bless you (Israel) and curses those that curse you."

God's promise (Abrahamic Covenant) is still in full effect. His prophets have proclaimed it down through history:

> *For thus says the Lord God: "Indeed I Myself will search for my sheep and seek them out. As a shepherd seeks out his flock on the day he is among his scattered sheep, so will I seek out My sheep and deliver them from all the places where they were scattered on a cloudy and dark day. And I will bring them out from the peoples and gather them from the countries and will bring them to their own land; I will feed them on the mountains of Israel, in the valleys and in all the inhabited places of the country.*

> *Ezekiel 34:11-13*

Moreover the word of the Lord came to me, saying: "Son of man, when the house of Israel dwelt in their own land, they defiled it by their own ways and deeds; to Me their way was like the uncleanness of a woman in her customary impurity. Therefore, I poured out my fury on them for the blood they had shed on the land, and for their idols with which they had defiled it. So, I scattered them among the nations, and they were dispersed throughout the countries; I judged them according to their ways and their deeds. When they came to the nations, wherever they went, they profaned my holy name-when they said of them, 'These are the people of the Lord, and yet they have gone out of His land.' But I had concern for My holy name, which the house of Israel had profaned among the nations wherever they went. Therefore, say to the house of Israel, 'Thus says the Lord God: I do not do this for your sake, O house of Israel, but for My holy name's sake, which you have profaned among the nations wherever you went. And I will sanctify My great name, which has been profaned among the nations, which you have profaned in their midst; and the nations shall know that I am the Lord," says the Lord God, "when I am hallowed in you before their eyes.

For I will take you from among the nations, gather you out of all countries, and bring you into your own land."

Ezekiel 36:16-24

God did not gather them to their own Land for their sake-He did it for His own name's sake. The Jews had profaned His name wherever they went, but God kept His promise so that all nations would know that "I AM the Lord." On May 14, 1948, the world saw what was believed to be impossible, Israel became a sovereign nation again after 2,000 years. It was impossible for man, *"but with God, all things are possible." Matthew 19:26*

PROPHECIES MADE	PROPHECIES FULFILLED
Acts 1:5 Jesus promised the Holy Spirit would come.	Acts 2:1-4 The apostles were filled with the Holy Spirit at Pentecost.
Isaiah 49:6 The message of the Gospel would come from the Jews to the Gentiles.	Acts 13:46-47 Because many Jews rejected the Gospel, Paul (a Jew) turned from preaching to the Jews to the Gentiles.
Ezekiel 34:11-13 God will gather His people from the nations and bring them back to Israel.	May 14, 1948 Israel became a sovereign nation.

QUESTIONS FOR DISCUSSION

People receive the Holy Spirit when they trust Christ for their salvation. Unless you became a Christian at a young age, you may remember what life was like for you before He came into your life. How has your life changed after receiving the Holy Spirit?

In the year 70 AD, God scattered the Jews around the world because they rejected Jesus as Messiah. While they were among the nations, most Jews dishonored God by their conduct. Why then would God bring them back to Israel?

CHAPTER 15: THE YEARS OF JUBILEE

The Lord spoke to Moses on Mount Sinai and Moses recorded His instructions in Leviticus 25. The children of Israel were about to enter the Promised Land and God wanted them to know how the land that He gave them should be treated. He told them that the land should keep a sabbath to the Lord. So, the land could be farmed as usual for six years but left fallow on the seventh.

The people were used to resting on the Sabbath day of the week to worship and rest, but it was a new command from the Lord to rest the land on the Sabbath (seventh) year. This practice would keep the land productive and in the seventh year, the people would not have to toil in their fields, thus giving them rest also. They were not to sow or reap during that year, but the crops that grew voluntarily on their own, the people and livestock could eat.

The year after the seven sabbaths of years was the year of Jubilee, the fiftieth year. The year of Jubilee began on the Day of Atonement of that year. The Day of Atonement or "Yom Kippur" was for the purpose of the people repenting of their sins in the past year and praying that God would forgive them. To usher in the Sabbath Year and the Year of Jubilee, a priest would blow the ram's horn (shepherd) on the Day of Atonement.

The year of Jubilee had a special meaning to the Jewish people. If land were sold during the previous 50 years, in the following year of Jubilee, the ownership of that land would revert back to the original owner. If sold, the price of the land would be determined by how many crops could be harvested before the next year of Jubilee. This reminded the people that the land ultimately belonged to God and all they were doing was "leasing" it from Him.

> *"The land shall not be sold permanently, **for the land is Mine**; for you are strangers and sojourners with Me. And in all the land of your possession you shall grant redemption of the land."*
>
> *Leviticus 25:23-24*

The main tenant of the year of Jubilee is the land would return to the original Jewish owner. The same could be said of the nation of Israel. Israel was taken out of existence in the year 70 AD when Titus, the Roman General destroyed the Temple and the city of Jerusalem. The people who were not killed were scattered to the far reaches of the world. But, according to the Abrahamic Covenant, the land was still owned by Israel. When a person or a nation dies they disintegrate and nothing is left. It is impossible for that process to be reversed, but *"with God all things are possible." Matthew 19:26*

Ezekiel chapter 37 is called the dry bones chapter. The question is asked: "Can these dry bones live?" meaning "Can Israel become a nation again? As Ezekiel watched and prophesied, the bones came together- "bone to bone." Then came the sinew, flesh and skin, but there was no breath in them. The Lord told Ezekiel to again prophesy to the breath to come from the four winds and breathe on these slain that they may live." (Ezekiel 37:9) So, they breathed and lived and stood on their feet-an exceeding great army.

> *"Then say to them,, 'Thus says the Lord God: "Surely I will take the children of Israel from among the nations, wherever they have gone, and will gather them from every side and bring them into their own land; and I will make them one nation in the land, on the mountains of Israel; and one king shall be king over them all; they shall no longer be two nations, nor shall they ever be divided into two kingdoms again.*
>
> *Ezekiel 37:21-22*

As was mentioned earlier, the main tenant of the year of Jubilee is that the Land would return to the original owner. Since 70 AD the land had "occupiers" living on the Land, but they did not own it in God's eyes. The last "occupier" of the Land was the Ottoman Empire who in 1517 defeated the Mamlukes in the Battle of Raydaniyah for the Land.

Seven Jubilees (350 years) after that battle was the year **1867**. That year the Ottoman Empire fought against Russia and others in the Crimean War. This was awfully expensive for the Ottoman Empire and it caused bankruptcy and necessitated the Empire to sell land. Jews from around the world began buying in large numbers. This event was prophesied by Jeremiah centuries before:

> *"Men will buy fields for money, sign deeds and seal them, and take witnesses in the land of Benjamin in the places around Jerusalem, in the cities of Judah, in the cities of the mountains, in the cities of the lowland and in the cities of the South; **for I will cause their captives to return, says the Lord**."*
>
> *Jeremiah 32:44*

Another amazing event took place in the Jubilee year of 1867. A British officer named Charles Warren was sent by Britain to survey ancient Jerusalem. This had to be done to prepare for the Jews who were beginning to come back in great numbers. This was also foretold in the book of Zechariah:

Charles Warren measured the Land. He envisioned the Jewish people learning again how to farm the Land and make it blossom. He saw how the Jews' return would lead to the birth of a nation. He believed that America and powerful nations of Europe would be involved in its resurrection which proved to be accurate.

Ever since 70 AD when the Jews were scattered around the world, they have been persecuted. It was to escape that persecution that **drove** them back to the Land and it was the dream of again living in the Land that **drew** them there.

The next Jubilee year after the Jubilee year of 1867 was, of course, 1917. God was working to return the Land back to the original owners, the Jewish people. That year Edmund Allenby was appointed general by the British to gain Land from the Ottoman Empire. On October 31, 1917, he fought and won the battle for Beersheba which set the tone for him to drive out the Ottoman Empire from the Land. It was because of Allenby's air force that the British was able to regain Jerusalem without any damage to the city.

The British air force was able to defeat the Ottoman Empire's air force making it possible for the British to control the skies over Jerusalem thus saving the city from damage. Centuries before, Isaiah wrote this prophecy:

> *"So, the Lord of hosts will come down to fight for Mount Zion and for its hill. Like birds flying about, so will the Lord of hosts defend Jerusalem. Defending, He will also deliver it; passing over, He will preserve it."*
>
> *Isaiah 31:4b-5*

That same year, the British foreign secretary, Arthur Balfour called for a draft to be made for a public declaration concerning the Land called the "Balfour Declaration". It declared,

> *His Majesty's Government views with favour the establishment in Palestine (the Land) of a national home for the Jewish people, and will use their best endeavours to facilitate the achievement of this object…*

Britain as a country was at the height of its power in 1917 because of its favorable treatment of the Jewish people ("I will bless those that bless you.") and Charles Warren, General Edmund Allenby and Arthur Balfour were sympathetic toward the plight of the Jews and wanted to help them.

During the first Jubilee in 1867 the Land was measured and in the second in 1917 it was transferred. The Jewish people then had tangible hope of a homeland and they continued to return in ever greater numbers.

As a review, the first year that launched the future years of Jubilee was **1517** when the Ottoman Empire defeated the Mamluks at the Battle of Raydaniyah. The Ottomans had occupied the land for 350 years (exactly 7 years of Jubilee). That brings us to the year of **1867**, the Ottoman Empire allowed Jews to purchase land, because of their massive debts and Charles Warren surveyed the ancient city of Jerusalem. Fifty years later in **1917**, through the military leadership of General Edmund Allenby, the British were able to drive out the Ottomans and Arthur Balfour drafted a declaration called the Balfour Declaration stating that Palestine would be a home for the Jewish People. The events of both Jubilee years, 1867 and 1917, encouraged the Jews to return to their Land. The Land was being returned to the original owners.

There was another fifty-year period that was essential to establishing the Jewish nation. In **1897**, Theodor Herzel, the founder of Zionism (Zion is another name for Jerusalem) attended the First Zionist Congress in Basel Switzerland. This conference was the beginning of the political movement that would lead to the creation of a

Jewish State. The exact date of this event was
August 31, 1897.

Fifty years later, the newly formed United Nations approved the Partition Plan which would give the Land back to the Jewish people and establish the nation of Israel. What was the date that the plan was completed? **August 31, 1947,** the exact date that the political movement to create a Jewish state, fifty years earlier. A Jubilee year which proves that God had His Hand in the process of bringing the Jews back to their Land and establishing Israel as a sovereign nation again.

> *"And you shall consecrate the fiftieth year…. It shall be a Jubilee for you; and each of you shall return to his possession."*
>
> *Leviticus 25:10*

Just as Charles Warren had predicted in 1867, for Israel to become a sovereign nation the backing of America would be needed. Harry S. Truman was chosen by President Roosevelt to be his Vice President. Roosevelt was president until his death in 1945 which made Truman the new president. Roosevelt was not in favor of the Jews having their own nation, but Truman was a Bible believing Christian and sympathized with the Jews' treatment during the Holocaust. He believed that they should go back to the Land and Israel should be a nation again. Truman threw his weight behind the formation of the Israeli state by giving it his sanction. America was the most powerful nation on earth after leading the Allies to victory over the Germans and the Japanese in World War II. By giving his approval, it guaranteed that the Jews would regain their country. In the spring of 1949, one year after Israel's birth, Israel's first Chief Rabbi, Isaac Herzog, came to America to visit President Truman. The Rabbi told the president that when he (President Truman) was in his mother's womb, the Lord had called him to be the instrument to bring about the rebirth of Israel after two thousand years.

In the late 1940's, the Jewish people came back to their Land in great numbers and on May 14, 1948 was reborn. They had regained their nation, but there was still something left to regain and that was their ancient capital-Jerusalem.

In 1917, the Land was transferred from the British to the Jewish People by the Balfour Declaration. That left the door open for God's children to return to Palestine. The Land had returned to its original owners-the Jews. In the **Jubilee year of 1967,** exactly fifty years after the Balfour Declaration they got their capital back. But it took winning a war to achieve it.

In May 1967 on the eve of Israel's anniversary, the Russians sent word to Egypt that Israel was about to attack Egypt. This report was false, but it prompted Egypt to put thousands of troops on Israel's borders.

Egypt then entered a military pact with Jordan and by the middle of June there were over 200,000 enemy troops on Israel's borders. Israel was out-gunned and our-manned. Nasser, the president of Egypt declared, "Our basic objective will be the destruction of Israel."

A great doom fell on Israel as coffins were stockpiled and public parks were designated to be cemeteries. Many feared that this would be the end of Israel. On June 3, 1967, the Israeli leaders decided to not wait to be attacked, but to attack their enemies first. So, on June 5, Israel's air force in a sudden strike, destroyed the air forces of all the surrounding Arab nations. When that was completed, the order was given to Colonel Motta Gur to take the old city. He led his men through the gate on the east side and for the first time in two thousand years, Israeli soldiers were standing on the streets of Jerusalem. Other soldiers swept down from the north onto the Temple Mount and Colonel Gur radioed the words to the nation, "The Temple Mount is in our hands." This was 1967, the year of Jubilee. Exactly 50 years since the Land was returned to the Jews in the Jubilee year of 1917 with the Balfour Declaration.

When Jerusalem was returned to the Jews in the Jubilee year of 1967, the world refused to recognize it as Israel's capital. In all its history, Jerusalem was always the capital of Israel. In the mid 1990's, the United States Congress passed a law calling for America's recognition of Jerusalem as capital of

Israel. However, the president signed a waiver which prevented that recognition. The waiver was signed every six months since until the **Jubilee year of 2017**. 2017 was the year that Donald Trump became president. It had been 50 years since Israel regained her capital during the Six Day War of 1967. President Trump signed the proclamation and the Senate passed the resolution in the year of the Jubilee-fifty years since the Six Day War.

God had promised repeatedly that He would bring His people back to their Land and establish Israel as a Nation. On one day, May 14, 1948 against all odds, He did it. Praise His Holy Name!

"Who has heard such a thing? Shall the earth be made to give birth in one day? Or shall a nation be born at once? For as soon as Zion was in labor, she gave birth to her children. Shall I bring to the time of birth, and not cause delivery? Says the Lord." Isaiah 66:8

PROPHECIES MADE	PROPHECIES FULFILLED
Ezekiel 37:21-22 God will bring the Jews back to their land and they will be one nation.	May 14, 1948 God brought them back to become one nation-Israel.
Isaiah 31:4b-5 God will defend, deliver and preserve Jerusalem.	1917 Allenby's air force protected Jerusalem from destruction.

Why did God bless the British in 2017 and America in 1947?

Why did God use the 50-year Jubilees in the process of fulfilling His promises to bring the Jews back to their Land?

CHAPTER 16: THE RAPTURE

Our wonderful Savior, Jesus, has many names to describe His character. At His First Coming, He was called The Lamb of God. Like the Passover lambs, He too was slain to take away our sins. Isaiah perfectly describes Him:

> *"He was oppressed, and He was afflicted, yet He opened not His mouth; He was led as a lamb to the slaughter, and as a sheep before its shearers is silent, so He opened not His mouth.*
>
> *Isaiah 53:7*

Jesus willingly went to the cross just as a lamb goes to slaughter. He did it because He loves the whole world. On the cross He took the punishment that we deserve so that those that trust Him for their salvation will not have to experience the horrors of eternal hell.

People, especially our generation, love *that* Jesus, but there is another Name for Jesus that you rarely hear- "The Lion of Judah." At the end of Daniel's 70th week (seven years), Jesus will return to bring His wrath to those that want to wage war against God and His People, the Jews. Leading up to that event will be the period of time called the Tribulation (Daniel's 70th week), the seven-year period that God will bring punishment upon the earth for their rejection of His Son. Most churches today do not teach about sin or hell and you rarely hear anything about the coming Tribulation on the earth. The description of the Tribulation is so horrific that people just do not want to think about it if they have any knowledge of it at all. Like the days of Noah, most people just want to go about their daily lives and not think about the calamity about to overwhelm them. But this time *will* come upon the earth.

> *"For behold, the Lord comes out of His place to **punish** the inhabitants of the earth for their iniquity; the earth will also disclose her bloodshed and will no more cover her slain."*
>
> *Isaiah 26:21*

God will never punish those that have received Jesus as their Savior. One definition for the word "punish" is "to inflict a penalty on someone as a retribution for an offense, especially a transgression." As Christians, our transgressions were dealt with on the cross so there is no need for God to punish us for something that no longer exists.

However, God will discipline us when we sin. Just as punishment will cause pain, so does discipline, but the goal of discipline is to make us better. God loves us and wants us to grow into the image of his Son. When we sin, He uses the pain of discipline to "get our attention" and cause us to repent from that sin so our fellowship with Him is restored when He forgives us. We should use discipline to train our own children because we love them as God loves us.

So how do Christians that are alive just prior to the beginning of the Tribulation escape the punishment that God will visit upon the earth? God will provide the Rapture, a supernatural event where people who have died in Christ will be raised from their graves and Christians who are alive will be "caught up" to meet Christ in the "air." The church will be taken to heaven to escape God's wrath on the earth.

> *"…wait for His Son from heaven, whom He raised from the dead, even Jesus who delivers us from the wrath to come."*
>
> *1 Thessalonians 1:10*

Pentecost was the beginning of the Church Age and the Rapture will be the end of it because the church will no longer be on the earth, but in Heaven.

Many today no longer believe that the Rapture will be in the church's future. Paul wrote about the Rapture in 1 Corinthians and 1 Thessalonians.

> *"Behold, I tell you a mystery; We shall not all sleep, but we shall all be changed-in a moment, in the twinkling of an eye, at the last trumpet. 'For the trumpet will sound, and the dead will be raised incorruptible, and we shall be changed. For this corruptible must put on incorruption, and this mortal must put on*

immortality. So, when this corruptible has put on incorruption, and this mortal has put on immortality, then shall be brought to pass the saying that is written: 'Death is swallowed up in victory. O Death, where is your sting? O Hades, where is your victory?"

1 Corinthians 15:51-55

In this passage, Paul talks about the suddenness of the Rapture. It will be like the blink of an eye that the dead (in Christ) will be raised with new bodies and those that are alive will be changed to have immortal bodies so that we all will have bodies suited for a heavenly existence.

*"But I do not want you to be ignorant, brethren, concerning those who have fallen asleep, lest you sorrow as others who have no hope. For if we believe that Jesus died and rose again, even so **God will bring with Him those who sleep in Jesus.** For this we say to you by the word of the Lord, that we who are alive and remain until the coming of the Lord will by no means precede those who are asleep. For the Lord Himself will descend from heaven with a shout, with the voice of an archangel, and the trumpet of God.*

*And the dead in Christ will rise first. Then we who are alive and remain shall be **caught up** together with them in the clouds to meet the Lord in the air. And thus, we shall always be with the Lord."*

1 Thessalonians 4:13-17

Paul did not want us to be uninformed about the Rapture. He wanted the people of Thessalonica to understand that their Christian friends and family who died (sleep) will be raised on the day of the Rapture. He also wanted them to understand that "to be absent from the body and to be present with the Lord" (2 Cor 5:8) is preferable than being here on earth. This infers that when our bodies die, we will immediately be with the Lord. So, at the Rapture Jesus will bring the souls of those who were in Christ to meet their now incorruptible bodies in the air. Those who are still living at the Rapture will be changed and will be "caught up" with the ones who were raised from their graves and all will meet our Lord in the air to be taken to Heaven.

Some do not believe in the Rapture because the word "Rapture" is not in the Bible which is true. The word "caught up" in verse 17, is translated from the Latin word rapturo, from which the term "Rapture" comes. In the Greek it is harpazo. So, the word (rapture) is not in the Bible, but the meaning certainly is.

The term *imminent* literally means "ready to take place." The New Testament teaches that the Rapture is imminent-nothing else must take place before Jesus meets his saints in the air. In my view, the last prophecy that had to be fulfilled was the return of the Jews to their Land and Israel become a sovereign nation. There is nothing else that God must accomplish before the rapture can occur. The fact that it could happen anytime now should motivate the church (us) to live lives that are pleasing to the Lord.

> *'The fact that the glorified, holy Son of God could step through the door of heaven at any moment is intended by God to be the most pressing, incessant, motivation for holy living and aggressive ministry (including missions, evangelism and Bible teaching) and the greatest cure for lethargy and apathy. It should make a difference in every Christian's values, actions, priorities and goals."*

> *Arnold Fruchtenbaum, The Footsteps of the Messiah*

Just knowing that there will be a future tribulation ought to motivate Christians to throw out a life jacket to our unsaved neighbors and friends. We know that we will not have to experience the tribulation, but what about the ones we love? If we *really* believe that the rapture is imminent and following the rapture is the worst seven years in the history of mankind and by leading them to Jesus they could be spared from that horror, wouldn't we want to share the Gospel with them?

And what about us? Every Christian should ask himself (me too!), "Do we really believe that this world is not our home?" If it is not, how should we be living knowing that any micro-second we could be looking into the face of Jesus? Paul put it this way:

"For our citizenship is in heaven, from which we also eagerly wait for the Savior, the Lord Jesus Christ, who will transform our lowly body that it may be conformed to His glorious body, according to the working by which He is able even to subdue all things to Himself."

Philippians 3:20-21

Many (as I have stated before) believe that the rapture is something out of science fiction. We believe it, but do we act like it? Paul wrote to Titus:

"...denying ungodliness and worldly lusts, we should live soberly, righteously, and godly in the present age, looking for the blessed hope and glorious appearing of our great God and Savior Jesus Christ."

Titus 2:12-13

As Christians, we have a fantastic future. God has given us the wonderful gift of knowing Him while we are on this earth, but we do not want to get caught up in the things of this world. We want to look up to our "blessed hope" so that when we are "caught up" we can look into his wonderful face and not be ashamed.

PROPHECIES MADE	PROPHECIES FULFILLED
Isaiah 26:21 God will punish the inhabitants of the earth for their iniquity. 1 Thessalonians 4:13-17 The Church will be taken to Heaven at the Rapture.	Daniel 12:1 Yet to be fulfilled in the Tribulation. Yet to be fulfilled at the Rapture

QUESTIONS FOR DISCUSSION

Are you looking forward to meeting Christ in the air
at the Rapture? Why or why not?

Do you know anyone who believes that the Rapture
is imminent? Do you?

If you do, has it changed the way you live?

CHAPTER 17: JUDGEMENT SEAT OF CHRIST

Jesus promised that He would come again to receive us unto Himself. This will be done at the Rapture when the dead in Christ will be raised incorruptible to meet Him in the air and Christians that are still living at that time will be changed so that they have new perfect bodies like His.

> *"Let not your heart be troubled; you believe in God, believe also in Me. In My Father's house are many mansions, if it were not so, I would have told you. I go to prepare a place for you. And if I go and prepare a place for you, I will come again and receive you to Myself; that where I am, there you may be also."*
>
> *John 14:1-3*

After the Rapture we will be led to Heaven by our Savior, but what happens then? Many Bible scholars believe that the Rapture will be followed by the Judgement. The Judgement Seat of Christ, sometimes called the Bema Seat, will be where Christians are judged by Jesus not for salvation (that has been decided and can never be changed), but for the works we have done while we lived on the earth. The Bema Seat was used at ancient Olympic events where an official awarded prizes to the race winners. The Bema Seat of Christ will be similar except for the possibility that rewards can be lost. In First Corinthians 3, Paul gives a picture of what that scene will look like:

> *For no other foundation can anyone lay than that which is laid, which is Jesus Christ. Now if anyone builds on this foundation with gold, silver, precious stones, wood, hay, straw, each one's work will become clear; for the Day will declare it, because it will be revealed by fire; and the fire will test each one's work, of what sort it is. If anyone's work which he has built on it endures, he will receive a reward. If anyone's work is burned, he will suffer loss; but he himself will be saved, yet so as through fire.*
>
> *1 Corinthians 3:11-15*

Verse eleven is the most critical in this passage. Our Foundation must be Jesus or nothing that follows has any meaning. The Foundation is stable and secure. If we have Jesus as our Foundation nothing can remove it from us. If we did not have this Foundation, when Jesus judges from the Bema, we would still be on earth facing a horrific seven years of Tribulation. The Bema Seat of Christ is a measure of how well we built upon that Foundation while we are on earth. Anything done in our own flesh will have no value (wood, hay, straw). But for the deeds that were done through the power of the Holy Spirit there will be great rewards.

While we are on the earth, we have a window of opportunity to build upon that Foundation. Paul said there are six building materials we can use to build: gold, silver precious stones or wood hay or straw. The first three are fireproof, but the last three are highly combustible.

Charles Swindoll has described this event like a dump truck that is loaded with all our works after we became Christians. The truck will back up to the Bema Seat and all our works are dumped out. Our works are then tested by fire. The wood, hay and straw representing the deeds we did in our flesh burn up. The gold, silver and precious stones are the works that we did through the power of the Holy Spirit. They are fireproof and eternal. We will suffer loss for the things that burn up, but we will gain rewards for the works that endure.

If anyone's works are completely burned up, he will suffer great loss, but "he himself will be saved" because he had the right "Foundation" that can never be burned up or lost, Jesus Himself.

Jesus encourages us in John 15 to "abide" in Him:

> *"Abide in Me, and I in you. As the branch cannot bear fruit of itself, unless it abides in the vine, neither can you, unless you abide in Me. I am the vine; you are the branches. He who abides in Me, and I in him, bears much fruit; for without Me you can do nothing."*

It is only when we are abiding in Christ that we do the works of gold, silver and precious stones. The more we abide in Him the more rewards we will receive from the hands of Jesus on that Day. Jeremiah wrote that even our thoughts and motives will be judged.

> *I, the Lord, search the heart, I test the mind, even to give every man according to his ways, according to the fruit of his doings.*
>
> *Jeremiah 17:10*

Perhaps we can all remember when we were children, our dad may have told us as he went to work to have the yard mowed before he came back home. We may have become busy with something else and forgot to mow the yard (or just decided we didn't want to). Then as he pulled in the driveway, we suddenly remembered and were ashamed that we disobeyed. We knew that there would be consequences! John wrote that there is the potential for all of us to feel that shame at the Bema seat.

> *"And now little children, abide in Him, that when He appears, we may have confidence and not be ashamed before Him at His coming."*
>
> *1 John 4:28*

There will be some that are genuinely saved, but will only have the ashes of wood, hay and straw to offer our Lord. They will be ashamed and suffer great loss. They will have no rewards, but they themselves will be saved "as though through fire." What a great motivation to abide in Him daily. None of us want to be ashamed when we come into His Holy presence. Toward the end of Paul's life, he summarized his service to Jesus,

> *"I have fought the good fight, I have finished the race, I have kept the faith. Finally, there is laid up for me the crown of righteousness, which the Lord, the righteous Judge, will give to me on that Day, and not to me only but also to all who have loved His appearing."*
>
> *2 Timothy 4:7-8*

At the Judgement (Bema) Seat of Christ, Jesus will righteously judge His Church. Some, like the Apostle Paul will receive great rewards, while others will have a loss of rewards. Today, there are Christians living only for themselves that will be ashamed to enter into His presence and others looking forward with great anticipation to His coming because they are "abiding" in Him.

PROPHECIES MADE	PROPHECIES FULFILLED
John 14:1-3 Jesus promised to come back for us	Yet to be fulfilled Will be fulfilled at the Rapture
2 Timothy 4:8 To all those who "love His appearing" Jesus will give a Crown of Righteousness	Yet to be fulfilled Will be fulfilled at the Judgement Seat of Christ

How important is it for Christians to understand that they will be judged for what they think and do while on this earth?

Does knowing that Jesus will one Day judge our motives, thoughts and actions bring you fear or great joy?

CHAPTER 18: THE INVASION OF ISRAEL

The invasion of Israel is prophesied in the book of Ezekiel. **It will happen (Ezekiel 39:8).** There are many good Bible scholars that disagree when this event will take place. What follows is what I believe God has presented in His Word. This narrative made the most sense to me as I studied the text and read books and commentaries on the subject. That being said, I may be wrong about the timing of these events. The important thing to remember is that God's timing is perfect. He is sovereign and fully in control. Time will tell who is right and who is wrong concerning this invasion. God knows and that is what matters the most.

Twenty-six hundred years ago, Ezekiel prophesied that at some future time Israel would be invaded by a coalition of nations. This event is recorded in Ezekiel 38-39. Many Biblical scholars believe that it will come about after the Rapture, but before the Tribulation begins. For reasons that will be explained later in this chapter, there could be months or several years following the Rapture before the Tribulation begins. At that time, Israel will have been a sovereign nation since 1948. She has to date swiftly won four major wars with her enemies, has a strong army and air force and is confident that she can repel any invasion from the Arab states. She is living "safely" in the land that God brought them to from many nations.

The coalition of nations will look upon Israel and say:

> *"I will go up against a land of unwalled villages; I will go to a peaceful people, who dwell safely, all of them dwelling without walls, and having neither bars nor gates to take plunder and to take booty, to stretch out your hand against the waste places that are again inhabited, and against a people gathered from the nations, who have acquired livestock and goods, who dwell in the midst of the land".*
>
> *Ezekiel 38:11-12*

This overwhelming force of nations is thought to include Russia and the "stan" countries which once made up the southern republics of the Soviet Union. Also included could be Turkey, Iran, Sudan, Libya and some other nations. This coalition of nations will look upon the wealth of Israel and covet those riches for themselves. Plus, this invasion would completely wipe out the Jewish nation which is the goal of many Arab countries. As strange as it may seem, God will drive them to invade.

> *"I (God) will turn you (the coalition of invading nations) around, put hooks into your jaws, and lead you out, with all your army, horses, and horsemen, all splendidly clothed, a great*

company with bucklers and shields, all of them handling swords.

Ezekiel 38:4

Why would God who loves his Chosen People, send a great army out against them? God's ways are not our ways and as we shall see, there are many reasons, but the main one is to show His power to protect them!

"I will set My Glory among the nations; all the nations shall see My judgment which I have executed, and My hand which I have laid on them. So, the house of Israel shall know that I am the Lord their God from that day forward."

Ezekiel 39:21-22

This invasion will likely take place after the Rapture but before the beginning of the Tribulation. One good reason for the possibility of this timing is that the United States, historically a staunch Israeli ally, would be severely weakened by the Rapture which will have taken many Israeli supporting Christians to heaven. This would give the coalition boldness to invade, knowing that America would likely not interfere with them. Indeed, in verse 13 of Chapter 38, several countries (probably including the US) will ask the coalition what their intentions are but do nothing about it.

Ezekiel describes the invasion in verses 14-16:

Therefore, son of man, prophesy and say to Gog (the coalition leader), "Thus says the Lord God: On that day when My people Israel dwell safely, will you not know it? Then you will come from your place out of the far north (Russia is straight north of Israel), you and many peoples with you, all of them riding on horses, a great company and a mighty army. You will come up against My people Israel like a cloud, to cover the land. It will be in the latter days that I will bring you against My land, so that the nations may know Me, when I am hallowed in you, O Gog, before their eyes."

Ezekiel 38:14-16

Unless God steps in to protect His People, Israel will be destroyed. There is no way that Israel can possibly repel such a large force against them. They will be standing alone with no other country to give them any protection. Israel must look to God in this impossible situation. And God will show up!

In His great anger against Gog, God will send a great earthquake in the land of Israel that shall be felt around the world. Verse 21 states that "every man's sword will be against his brother. Israel's enemies will kill each other! The following verses describes how God will use the weather and pestilence to plummet the coalition. He will send flooding rain, great hailstones, fire and brimstone. God will devastate the coalition of wicked nations.

*"Thus, I will magnify Myself and sanctify
Myself, and I will be known in the eyes of
many nations. Then they shall know that I am
the Lord.*

Ezekiel 38:23

Ron Rhodes, a well-known seminary professor at
Dallas Theological Seminary writes in his book, The
End Times in Chronological Order (page 81):

> *What a turn of events all this will be. The
> invading troops will come with the intention of
> killing, but they themselves will be killed. They
> will believe their power is overwhelming, but
> they will be overwhelmed by the greater power
> of God. They will come to take over a new
> land (Israel) but instead will be buried in the
> land.*

> *Behold, He who keeps Israel shall neither
> slumber nor sleep.*

> *Psalms 121:4*

Not only is the coalition's army completely
decimated, but at least some of their homelands are
destroyed. Verse 6 of chapter 39 states:

> *And I will send fire on Magog (the land of Gog)
> and on those who live in security in the
> coastlands.*

Then they shall know that I am the Lord.

Ezekiel 39:6

Little will these wicked nations realize that Israel is God's chosen people whom He loves. When they attack Israel, they are attacking God and He will deal with them severely. Indeed, there will be such a vast number of dead that it will take seven months for Israel to bury them. For the next seven years, Israel will burn the weapons of their enemies. They will have no need to burn their own fuel.

> *"Then those who dwell in the cities of Israel will go out and set on fire and burn the weapons, both the shields and bucklers, the bows and arrows, the javelins and spears; and they will make fires with them **for seven years**. …and they will plunder those who plundered them, and pillage those who pillaged them," says the Lord.*

Ezekiel 39:9-10b

In Matthew 24, Jesus urges the Jews living in Jerusalem to take flight when the antichrist sets up his headquarters there in the middle of the Tribulation. Since the Tribulation lasts for seven years, the middle of it will have to be three and a half years after the antichrist signs a covenant with Israel, which marks the beginning of the Tribulation. It makes sense then that if the invasion begins after the Rapture, there will have to be at least three and a half years before the Tribulation begins, because at the middle of the Tribulation (three and a half years later) the Jew will flee Jerusalem. So, burning the weapons will happen three and a half years **before** the Tribulation begins and three and a half years **after** it begins for a total of seven years as indicated in verse 9.

Ron Rhodes, in his book, wrote about the reasons for God's destruction of the wicked nations that made up the coalition.

> *Clearly, God's destruction of the northern invaders will be a powerful testimony that no one can ignore. Indeed, the whole world will witness God's destruction of the invaders and recognize His greatness, holiness, and glory (Ezekiel 38:23; 39:13,21). Moreover, Israel will be utterly awed at God's intervention on its behalf. God's stunning defeat of Gog and his military machine will force Israel to acknowledge His unfathomable power and justice. Page 84 "The End Times in Chronological Order"*

> *"When I have brought the back from the peoples and gathered them out of their enemies' lands, and I am hallowed in them in the sight of many nations, then they shall know that I am the Lord their God, who sent them into captivity among the nations, but also brought them back to their land and left none*

Russia's army along with the Muslim countries' armies that made up the coalition will be decimated by God when they try to invade Israel. When that happens, the balance of power of the world will shift and will allow the antichrist to rise to power. Israel will forget that it is God who protects her. Instead, they will trust the antichrist to protect them. He will sign the seven-year peace covenant with Israel. This will mark the beginning of the Tribulation which will be Daniel's 70th week. Because they will have little interference from Muslim countries, Israel will build her Temple within a matter of months on the Temple Mount and sacrifices will begin again. Three and one-half years after signing the peace treaty, the antichrist will set up an abominable idol (the abomination of desolation) in the Temple. He will terminate worship there and all hell will break loose upon the Jewish people thus breaking his peace covenant with Israel. Jesus described these events:

will be great tribulation, such as has not been since the beginning of the world until this time, no, nor ever shall be.

Matthew 24:15-16, 21

PROPHECIES MADE	PROPHECIES FULFILLED
Ezekiel: 38:11-12 Israel will be invaded by a coalition of armies from many Nations	Not yet fulfilled
Ezekiel 38:18-23 God will destroy the invading armies of the "north"	Not yet fulfilled

Why would God bring the coalition of armies against the land and people that He loves? Ezekiel 38:16

When Israel realizes that God has protected her, why does she feel the need to sign a peace covenant with the antichrist?

CHAPTER 19: THE TRIBULATION AND THE ANTICHRIST

The Bible reveals that the single event that triggers the seven-year Tribulation is the signing of the peace covenant between Israel and the antichrist. The events described in Daniel 9:24-27 lay out a prophetic timetable for the nation of Israel. According to the text, this timetable is divided up into 70 groups (weeks) of seven years or 490 years. These 490 years are split into two periods-483 years and 7 years.

1. The first period of 483 years began when Artaxerxes' sent Nehemiah to rebuild the walls in Jerusalem.
2. The first period (to the day) ended when Jesus Christ, the Messiah, rode into Jerusalem on a donkey.
3. Jesus died on the cross and in AD 70 the Temple and the city of Jerusalem were leveled.
4. The church age began at Pentecost (God sent the Holy Spirit to His church) and will end when God takes His church to Heaven at the Rapture.
5. The second period (7 years) will begin when antichrist makes a peace covenant with Israel. This is the seven-year Tribulation, "Daniel's

70th week." During the first half of the Tribulation, Israel will build her Temple.

6. Three and one-half years into the Tribulation the antichrist will break his covenant with Israel by setting up an abominable idol (an image of himself) in the Temple and will terminate worship of the true God there. Terrible persecution of the Jews will begin at that point.

7. Three and one-half years after the antichrist takes over the Temple in Jerusalem, Jesus Christ will return to earth and send the antichrist to hell.

The seven-year Tribulation will be the worst time that the world has ever experienced. Indeed, Jesus warned:

> *"For then there will be great tribulation, such as has not been since the beginning of the world until this time, no, nor ever shall be. And unless those days were shortened, no flesh would be saved; but for the elect's (believers that accept Christ after the Tribulation begins) sake those days will be shortened.*
>
> *Matthew 24:21-22*

Because of the Rapture, the church will not have to experience any part of the Tribulation. But it is good for pre-raptured Christians to understand some basic facts about what lies ahead for those unsaved individuals with whom we come in contact every day.

The apostle John wrote:

> *Blessed is he who reads and those who hear the words of this prophecy (the book of Revelation) and keep those things which are written in it; for the time is near (imminent).*
>
> *Revelation 1:3*

If God had not wanted Christians to read and understand (as much as we can) Revelation, He would not have included it in the Bible. He wants us to recognize that there will come a time when our unbelieving friends, neighbors and family will have to face the Tribulation and/or Hell itself. That fact should motivate us to share the Gospel with them so they can not only avoid the Tribulation/Hell but be able to enjoy all the pleasures of Heaven with us. Also, by knowing something about things to come, Christians should be encouraged to live Holy lives apart from the world.

Most churches today want only to believe in a God of love, which He is. But equally important to recognize is that He also brings wrath upon the world-especially at the Tribulation. Zephaniah prophesied in his book:

God will punish those that reject His Son. It is true that some who missed the Rapture will trust Christ and have their sins forgiven, but others will shake their fists at God and have nothing to do with His Free Gift of Salvation. Many Jews will also recognize that Jesus, the one they rejected, is the true Messiah. In fact, during the Tribulation, "a great multitude which no one could number" will come to a saving knowledge of Jesus because of the testimony of 144,000 Jewish evangelists (Revelation 7:9-14). This will be the greatest revival the world has ever seen. Unfortunately, many will be martyred by the antichrist for their faith. The new Christians that do live through the Tribulation will enter the Millennium at the Second Coming of Christ.

The Book of Revelation describes what the earth will have to endure during the Tribulation. Ron Rhodes comments on these terrible conditions:

*"Human suffering will steadily escalate
throughout the tribulation period. First come*

God's seal judgments, involving bloodshed,
famine, death, economic upheaval, a great
earthquake, and cosmic disturbances
(Revelation 6) Then come His trumpet
judgments, involving hail and fire mixed with
blood, the sea turning to blood, water turning
bitter, further cosmic disturbances, affliction by
demonic scorpions, and the death of a third of
humankind (Revelation 8:8-9:21). Finally come
His increasingly worse bowl judgments,
involving horribly painful sores on human
beings, more bodies of water turning to blood,
the death of all sea creatures, people being
scorched by the sun, rivers drying up, total
darkness engulfing the land, a devastating
earthquake, widespread destruction, and
much more (Revelation 16). Such is the
judgement of God on a Christ-rejecting world."
Bible Prophecy Answer Book, Pages 131 and
132*

The apostle Paul warned of a "man of lawlessness"-
the antichrist:

*"Let no one deceive you by any means; for
that Day will not come unless the falling away
comes first, and the man of sin (lawlessness)
is revealed, the son of perdition, who opposes
and exalts himself above all that is called God
or that is worshiped, so that he sits as God in
the temple of God, showing himself that he is
God. The coming of the lawless one is*

*according to the working of Satan, with all power, signs and lying wonders, and with all unrighteous deception among those who perish because **they did not receive the love of the truth**, that they might be saved. And for this reason, God will send them **strong delusion**, that they should believe the lie, and they all may be condemned who did not believe the truth but had pleasure in unrighteousness."*

2 Thessalonians 2:3-4, 9-11

Paul's description of the antichrist shows much about his personality. First, Paul wanted to assure the Thessalonians that before the "Day" (Christ's return at the end of the Tribulation) that there would be a falling away. Some people will not receive the "love of the truth that they may be saved." As a result of this attitude, God will send them strong delusions that they should believe the lie. The antichrist will not be revealed until after the Rapture, but a foreshadowing of God sending strong delusions to people who will not believe in Him is apparent today. As we are seeing in our world and country today, there is a spirit of lawlessness and a spirit of antichrist that prevails.

We see not only approval of evil in our society, but those that encourage and applaud evil, calling evil "good." These are all signs that the Rapture is near!

When the antichrist is revealed, he will oppose God and exalt himself above God. As mentioned previously, He will show himself as God in the Jerusalem Temple. Like satan, he will have all powers, signs, and "lying wonders" with deception that will bring unrighteousness. He will be revealed at a time when the world is in a mess after the Rapture. He will be like satan who can appear as an "angel of light" but will be full of darkness. People will flock to him and believe that he is the Messiah. He will be extremely attractive and a smooth talker. His personality will be so magnetic that the whole world will beg to follow him, and he will lead the world to form a one-world government, something that all ruthless leaders of the world from Alexander the Great to Hitler himself were unable to do. When he obtains complete control of the world, he will show his true colors. In the book of Revelation, he is called the "beast" 32 times. This is because he will have "beast" like characteristics. He will make Hitler's persecution of the Jews look like a Sunday School picnic. He will behead newly converted Christians as fast as he can. He will have control of all commerce in that without the mark of the beast, no one will be able to buy or sell, causing many people to starve to death. He will have a "helper" called the false prophet that will do his bidding. The selection of this man will complete the unholy trinity-Satan, antichrist and the false prophet. The antichrist will most likely come out of Europe and some believe that the language in Daniel 9:27 points to the possibility that he will be a Roman.

Unlike Christ's reign over the whole world which will last eternally, the antichrist's reign will last only seven terrible years. Christ's return at the end of the Tribulation, both the antichrist and the false prophet will be thrown into the lake of fire which they will so richly deserve.

PROPHECIES MADE	PROPHECIES FULFILLED
Zephaniah 1:17 God will punish people who are alive in the Tribulation for rejecting His Son	Not yet fulfilled
2 Thessalonians 2:9-12 God will send "strong delusions" to those that "did not receive the love of the truth."	Partially Fulfilled The spirit of antichrist is already at work in our world today. Many people who have not received "the love of the truth" are already deluded.

QUESTIONS FOR DISCUSSION

Does God have the right to send punishment to those who reject His Son and live unrighteous lives?

What proof do we have that people who "have not received the love of the truth" are infected with "strong delusions" from God?

What is "the love of the truth."

CHAPTER 20: ARMAGEDDON & CHRIST'S SECOND COMING TO EARTH

Three and one-half years into the Tribulation, antichrist will desecrate the Temple and break his peace covenant with the Jews. Jesus warned in Matthew 24, when the Jews see these things take place, the inhabitants of Israel should leave quickly.

> *"Therefore when you see the 'abomination of desolation' (when antichrist sets himself up as god in the Temple), spoken of by Daniel the prophet, standing in the holy place (whoever reads, let him understand), then let those who are in Judea flee to the mountains. Let him who is on the housetop not go down to take anything out of his house. And let him who is in the field not go back to get his clothes. But woe to those who are pregnant and to those who are nursing babies in those days. And pray that your flight may not be in winter or on the Sabbath. For then there will be great tribulation, such as has not been since the beginning of the world until this time, no, nor ever shall be. And unless those days were shortened no flesh would be saved; but for the elect's sake those days will be shortened."*

> *Matthew 24:15-22*

Jesus knew that when antichrist, the lawless one, broke his peace agreement with Israel, intense persecution against the Jews would begin in earnest Many Jews will be killed by antichrist,but there will be a remnant that will escape to the "mountains" and be protected by God there.

> *"Then the woman (a metaphor referring to Israel) fled into the wilderness where she has a place prepared by God, that they should feed her there one thousand two hundred and sixty days (the last three and one-half years of the Tribulation). But the woman was given two wings of a great eagle, that she might fly into the wilderness to her place, where she is nourished for a time and times and half a time, from the presence of the serpent."*
>
> *Revelation 12:6,14*

So, just where are these "mountains" in the "wilderness" that God has prepared for His Jewish remnant? The Scriptures do not give us a crystal-clear answer to that question, but it does give us some strong indications of where this place of protection is located. There are passages that give us hints, when put together we can connect the dots and be fairly sure of this place of security. The first verse is in Daniel:

> *"He (antichrist) shall also enter the Glorious Land (Israel), and many countries shall be*

*overthrown; but these shall escape from his hand: **Edom, Moad**, and the prominent people of **Ammon**.”*

Daniel 11:41

Fruchtenbaum wrote in his book, "The Footsteps of the Messiah:

*"The passage (Daniel 11:41 states that while antichrist will conquer the whole world, there will be nations that escape his domination: **Edom, Moab** and **Ammon**. All three of these ancient nations currently comprise the single modern kingdom of **Jordan**." Arnold G. Fruchtenbaum, The Footsteps of Messiah, Page 29*

For some reason, the antichrist will be unable to overthrow Jordan. Could it be that God will spare Jordan from the domination of antichrist so that the remnant will have a place to go? Jordan is east of Israel, but the remnant could go straight south from Jerusalem and a little east and arrive in the Wilderness of Bozrah where the ancient city of Petra is located (see map). Petra was a scene in the 1981 American movie, "Raider of the Lost Ark" starring Harrison Ford. Many have seen that movie and are familiar with Petra (see photo), but not many realize that this could be the place that God will protect His Jewish remnant from antichrist during the second half of the Tribulation. The prophet Isaiah wrote in chapter 16:

*"Take counsel, execute judgment; make your shadow like the night in the middle of the day; hide the outcasts (the Jewish remnant), do not betray him who escapes. Let My outcasts dwell with you O **Moab (Jordan)**; be a shelter to them from the face of the spoiler (antchrist).*

Isaiah 16:3-4b

*"Who will bring me to the strong city? Who will lead me to **Edom (Jordan)**? Is it not You, O God, who cast us off? And You, O God, who did not go out with our armies? Give us help from trouble, for the help of man is useless. Through God we will do valiantly, for it is He who shall tread down our enemies."*

Psalms 108:10-13

"He will dwell on high (heights); His place of defense will be the fortress of rocks; bread will be given him; his water will be sure."

Isaiah 33:16

"Petra is located in a basin within Mount Seir and is totally surrounded by mountains and cliffs. The only way in and out of the city is through a narrow passageway (see photo) that extends for about a mile and can only be

*negotiated by foot or by horseback. This
makes the city easy to defend, and its
surrounding high cliffs give added meaning to
Isaiah 33:16 above. The name Bozrah means
"sheepfold." an ancient sheepfold had a
narrow entrance so that the shepherd could
count his sheep. Once inside the fold, the
sheep had more room to move around. Petra
is shaped like a giant sheepfold, with its
narrow passage opening up to a spacious
circle surrounded by cliffs." Fruchtenbaum,
The Footsteps of Messiah, pg 296-297*

One interesting sidelight: In Matthew 24:20 and
Mark 13:18, Jesus instructs the Jews to pray that
their flight to safety would not be in winter. This
could be because in winter travel would be more
difficult. But, there could be another reason why. In
Revelation 12 John wrote:

*"So, the serpent (satan) spewed water out of
his mouth like a flood after the woman (Israel)
that he might cause her to be carried away by
the flood. But the earth helped the woman
and the earth opened its mouth and swallowed
up the flood which the dragon had spewed out
of his mouth."*

Revelation 12:15-16

The narrow passage that leads to Petra has a flow of
water in the winter but is dry in the summer. Since

the Jewish remnant would have to travel through this passage, could this be the reason why Christ said to pray that their flight would not be in winter? Nevertheless, God will take care of His sheep and get them to safety.

2

Micah describes an assembly of Jacob (Israel), a remnant, which will be gathered into a fold (bozrah). The one who breaks them out is clearly a reference to Messiah, the Good Shepherd:

> *"I will surely assemble all of you O Jacob, I will surely gather the remnant of Israel; I will put them together like sheep of the fold, like a flock in the midst of their pasture; they shall make a loud noise because of so many people.*

[3] Čeština: Soutěska Al-Siq v Petře, Jordánsko. Picture by User:JoTB. Not modified. (https://commons.wikimedia.org/wiki/File:Al-Siq_2.jpg) Creative Commons Attribution-Share Alike 3.0 Unported (https://creativecommons.org/licenses/by-sa/3.0/deed.en)

The word Armageddon literally means "Mount of Megiddo" and is located about sixty miles north of Jerusalem. Historically, many battles have been fought at that location. The "Battle of Armageddon" probably should be called the "Campaign of Armageddon." It is more than just one battle shortly before the return of Jesus at the end of the Tribulation. It will be made up of a series of battles, **none** of which will be fought at the Armageddon location. This location will merely be a place that is large enough for armies from all over the world to **be gathered** by demons sent out by the unholy trio, saten, antichrist and the false prophet. The Euphrates River to the east will be dried up so that armies from the east will have an easier journey to the Armageddon location. Just as tyrants down through history tried to do, antichrist's goal will be to totally wipe out the Jewish people and their nation. In Revelation 16:14, John wrote:

"And I saw three unclean spirits like frogs coming out of the mouth of the dragon (satan), out of the mouth of the beast (antichrist) and out of the mouth of the false prophet. For they are spirits of demons, performing signs, which

go out to the kings of the earth and of the whole world, to gather them to the battle of that great day of God Almighty. And they gathered them together to the place called in Hebrew, Armageddon"

Revelation 16:13-14, 16.

Sometime during the second half of the Tribulation, antichrist will move to Babylon and rebuild it to be a worldwide economic and religious center. At that point, God will raise up a military force from the "north" to come down to destroy Babylon.

"Move from the midst of Babylon, go out of the land of the Chaldeans; and be like the rams before the flocks. For behold, I (God) will raise and cause to come up against Babylon an assembly of great nations from the north country. And they shall array themselves against her; from there she shall be captured. Their arrows shall be like those of an expert warrior. None shall return in vain. Because of the wrath of the Lord she (Babylon) shall not be inhabited, but she shall be wholly desolate. Everyone who goes by Babylon shall be horrified and hiss at all her plagues."

Jeremiah 50:8-9,13

Antichrist will not be in Babylon when this coalition from the north destroys the city. Instead of taking revenge on the armies that wipe out his capital, he will turn again to take it out on Jerusalem and this time Jerusalem will be plundered and thousands more Jews will be killed. Zechariah 14:2 adds this:

> *"I will gather **all** the nations against Jerusalem to battle, and the city shall be taken, and the houses plundered, and the women raped."*

> *And the dragon was enraged with the woman (Israel), and he went to make war with the rest of her offspring, who keep the commandments of God and have the testimony of Jesus Christ.*

> *Revelation 12:17*

As mentioned earlier, many Jews will flee Jerusalem when antichrist first comes to Jerusalem and set himself up as god in the Temple half way through the Tribulation. It is this remnant of Jews that will flee to the south of Jerusalem to (probably) Petra (located in the wilderness of Bozrah in Jordan) that antichrist will turn to next. His intentions will be to finally complete his genocide of the Jews. But God will protect His remnant.

Now with two-thirds of the Jewish population dead, and the armies from every country of the world poised to kill God's remnant, Israel's blindness will be lifted and they will cry out to the Lord and recognize that Jesus, the one they crucified, was indeed their Messiah. Hosea prophesied that Israel's leaders will call for the remnant to repent:

"Come and let us return to the Lord; for He has torn, but He will heal us; He has stricken, but He will bind us up. After two days (of repenting) He will revive us; on the third day He will raise us up that we may live in His sight. Let us know, let us pursue the knowledge of the Lord. His going forth is established as the morning; He will come to us like the rain, like the latter and former rain to the earth."

Hosea 6:1-3

"And it shall come to pass in all the land," says the Lord, "that two-third shall be cut off and die, but one-third shall be left in it; I will bring the one-third through the fire, will refine them as silver is refined, and test them as gold is tested. They will call on My name, and I will answer them. I will say, 'This is My people,' and each one will say, 'The Lord is my God.'"

Zechariah 13:8-9

"And I will not hide My face from them anymore; for I shall have poured out My Spirit on the house of Israel, say the Lord God."

Ezekiel 39:29

The apostle Paul wrote about this day in the book of Romans:

"For I do not desire, brethren, that you should be ignorant of this mystery, lest you should be wise in your own opinion, that blindness in part has happened to Israel until the fullness of the Gentiles has come in. And so all Israel will be saved, as it is written: 'The Deliverer (Jesus) will come out of Zion, and He will turn away ungodliness from Jacob; for this is My covenant with them, when I take away their sins.'"

Romans 11:25-27

As the remnant of Israel repents and mourns for their true Savior, Jesus will return to earth to defend His people:

"It shall be in that day that I will seek to destroy all the nations that come against Jerusalem. And I will pour on the house of David and on the inhabitants of Jerusalem the Spirit of grace and supplication; then they will look on Me who they pierced. Yes, they will mourn for Him as one mourns for his only son and grieve for Him as one grieves for a firstborn."

Zechariah 12:9-10

Christ's second coming will not be missed by anyone living on the earth:

"Behold, He is coming with the clouds, and every eye will see Him, even they who pierced

Him. And all the tribes of the earth will mourn because of Him. Even so, Amen.

Revelation 1:7

Jesus described his coming in this way:

"Then the sign of the Son of Man will appear in heaven, and then all the tribes of the earth will mourn, and they will see the Son of Man coming on the clouds of heaven with power and great glory."

Matthew 24:30

We can scarcely imagine what the armies of antichrist felt when they looked up and saw the King of kings and Lord of lords coming to defend His remnant. John describes it this way:

"Now I saw heaven opened, and behold, a white horse. And He who sat on him was called Faithful and True and in righteousness He judges and makes war. His eyes were like a flame of fire, and on His head were many crowns. He had a name written that no one know except Himself. He was clothed with a robe dipped in blood, and His name is called The Word of God. And the armies in heaven, clothed in fine linen, white and clean, (His Raptured believers!) followed him on white horses. Now out of His mouth goes a sharp sword, that with it He should strike the nations.

And He Himself will rule them with a rod of iron. He Himself treads the winepress of the fierceness and wrath of Almighty God. And He has on His robe and on His thigh a name written: KING OF KINGS AND LORD OF LORDS."

Revelation 19:11-16

Verses 19-21 of Revelation 19 tells that Jesus will make war against antichrist and his army. The beast (antichrist) and the false prophet will be thrown into the lake of fire and the rest of antichrist's army will be killed with the sword which proceeds from the mouth of Jesus.

When our warrior Jesus fights against the nations of the world, He will be destroying those who sought to destroy His Jewish remnant. Antichrist's armies will want to fight against the Jews, but they soon will discover that they will have to fight against the One who loves His People. The mention of Him coming from Edom (Jordan) and Bozrah is further evidence that the place of security for Israel for the second half of the Tribulation very well can be Petra.

"Who is this who comes from Edom, with dyed garments from Bozrah, this One who is glorious in His apparel, traveling in the greatness of His strength?

"I who speak in righteousness, mighty to save."

"Why is your apparel red, and Your garments like one who treads in the winepress?"

"I have trodden the winepress alone, and from the peoples no one was with Me. For I have trodden them in My anger and trampled them in my fury; their blood is sprinkled upon My garments, and I have stained all My robes. For the day of vengeance is in My heart, and the year of My redeemed has come."

Isaiah 63:1-4

After His victory over antichrist and his army, Jesus will ascend to the Mount of Olives:

"Then the Lord will go forth and fight against those nations, as He fights in the day of battle. And in that day His feet will stand on the Mount of Olives, which faces Jerusalem on the east and the Mount of Olives shall be split in two from east to west, Making a very large valley, Half of the mountain shall move toward the north and half of it toward the south."

Zechariah 14:3-4

JUDGEMENT OF THE NATIONS

Christ's Second Coming will mark the end of the Tribulation. There are several "judgements" mentioned in the Bible. One that has already been discussed is the Judgement Seat of Christ or the

Bema Seat of Christ. At this judgement, Christ will judge believers based on their works while they lived on the earth. It will take place after the Rapture. If an individual's works counted for eternity, he will gain rewards (crowns). If he lived to please himself and did not live to "abide in Christ" he will lose rewards, but no one will lose their salvation. This judgement is not to decide who goes to heaven and who goes to hell.

After the Tribulation and the Second Coming of Christ, there will be another judgement. This one is called the Judgement of the Nations or the Sheep and Goats Judgement. Jesus describes this judgement in Matthew 25:31-46. Jesus will judge the Gentiles who lived on earth during the Tribulation and it will take place on earth. It will be based on how people treat "Christ's brothers." Some suggest that these "brothers" are the 144,000 Jewish evangelists that will have great success in bringing "a great multitude" to belief in Jesus.

During the Tribulation it will be extremely hard to get the necessities of life, especially for those that will not receive the Mark of the Beast. For those that will sacrifice their own meager belongings to share with the "brothers", Jesus will reward them with the privilege of entering into the Millennial Kingdom that is to follow. However, those that will not share with the "brothers", will go away into everlasting punishment while the righteous will have eternal life.

Jesus will consider the "brothers" so close to Himself that how others will treat them will be likened to how they will be treating Him. Evidence of this is His statement, "Truly, I say to you, as you did it to one of the least of these my brothers, you did it to me."

On the surface, this may appear to be salvation based on works. A deeper understanding of the situation they were in shows that it is not. *The Bible Knowledge Commentary* provides the evidence:

> *"A Gentile going out of his way to assist a Jew in the Tribulation will mean the Gentile has become a believer in Jesus Christ during the Tribulation.* ***By such a stand and action, a believing Gentile will put his life in jeopardy. His works will not save him; but his works will reveal that he is redeemed."***

As a reminder, any true Christian reading this chapter before the Rapture will not be judged at this time. Christians whether the dead in Christ or those living at the time of the Rapture will be judged for rewards at the Judgement Seat of Christ. When the Tribulation is on the earth, all who are Christians at the Rapture will be in Heaven and will return with Christ at His Second Coming.

PROPHECIES MADE	PROPHECIES FULFILLED
Matthew 24:15-17 When antichrist desecrates the Temple, run for the mountains.	Revelation 12:6,14 Yet to be fulfilled. A Jewish remnant flees to the wilderness to a place prepared by God.
Zechariah 13:8-9 After much testing, the Jewish Remnant will turn back to God.	Romans 12:25-27 Yet to be fulfilled. Because of God's Covenant with them, He will take away their sins.
Matthew 24:30 Jesus will come on the clouds of Heaven with power and great Glory.	Revelation 19:11-16 Yet to be fulfilled. Jesus will come on a white horse to strike the nations.

QUESTIONS FOR DISCUSSION

Why is it so vital that Christ save a remnant of Jews out of the Tribulation?

What other time(s) in Israel's history has God defended His People when their enemy was closing in to annihilate them?

Do you find it ironic that God will gather up the army "from the North" to destroy Babylon, while demons will gather the world army to destroy the Jews? Why?

CHAPTER 21: MARRIAGE SUPPER OF THE LAMB

Based on Daniel 12:11-13, there is evidence that there will be a seventy-five-day interval between the end of the Tribulation and the beginning of the Millennial Kingdom. During this interlude, it is believed that several important events will transpire.

1. The antichrist and the false prophet will be cast into the Lake of Fire. "The beast was captured and with it the false prophet…were thrown into the lake of fire that burns with sulfur." Revelation 19:20. They will burn there forever.
2. Satan will be bound until the end of the Millennial Kingdom. Revelation 20:1-3 states that an angel will come down from Heaven with the keys to the bottomless pit. He will seize the devil and throw him into the pit for a thousand years so he will not be able to deceive the nations.
3. The saints who will have become Christians during the Tribulation and will be subsequently martyred will be resurrected and reign with Christ for a thousand years. Revelation 20:4
4. It is quite possible that toward the end of this seventy-five-day period, the marriage feast of Christ will be celebrated.

To understand the background of Christ's marriage feast, it is necessary to have some knowledge about the traditions of the Jewish wedding. First, the marriage was legally consummated by the parents of the bride and groom. Then the groom went to prepare a place for the bride and groom to live which was an addition to his father's house. When he was finished with the construction of their dwelling, the groom came to claim his bride. The bride had to be ready because she did not know when the groom would come to take her to the marriage supper that could last several days. All three phases of the Jewish wedding are seen in Christ's relationship to the Church, the bride of Christ.

As individuals trust Christ for their salvation, they become members of the church, the bride of Christ. Meanwhile, Christ, the Bridegroom is preparing a place for the bride of Christ in His Father's house in Heaven. The Bridegroom then will come to claim his bride (the church) at the Rapture and take her to Heaven. The actual marriage will take place in heaven prior to the second coming at the end of the Tribulation. The Marriage supper of the Lamb will follow the second coming, apparently taking place toward the end of the interlude that is between the Second Coming and the beginning of the Millennial Kingdom.

> *"We can see other parallels as well. Just as ancient Jewish grooms paid a purchase price to establish the marriage covenant, so Jesus*

paid a purchase price for the church (His precious blood). Also, just as a Jewish bride was declared sanctified or set apart in waiting for her groom, so the church is declared sanctified and set apart for Christ the Bridegroom. And just as a Jewish bride was unaware of the exact time her groom would come for her, so the church is unaware of the exact time that Jesus the Bridegroom will come, though it is an imminent event."

Ron Rhodes, The End Times in Chronological Order, Pages 47-48.

"Let not your heart be troubled; you believe in God, believe also in Me. In My father's house are many mansions; if it were not so, I would have told you. I go to prepare a place for you. And if I go and prepare a place for you, I will come again and receive you to Myself; that where I am, there you may be also."

John 14:1-3

Following the Second Coming of Christ, the Millennial Kingdom will begin on earth. Who will be there and what will it be like? We know that all true Christians will be taken from the earth at the Rapture, but there will be people that come to Christ during the Tribulation-both Gentiles and Jews. Those are the mortal people that will be invited by Jesus to enter his one-thousand-year kingdom on earth.

People in Christ's Kingdom will live much longer than in this present age.

> *"No more shall an infant from there live but a few days, nor an old man who has not fulfilled his days; for the child shall die one hundred years old…."*
>
> *Isaiah 65:20a*

However, because they will be mortal, they will grow old and die. People will marry and have babies. Unfortunately, some of these children will reject Christ in their hearts while still obeying Him. Some of these people born into the Kingdom will revolt against God at the end of the Millennium when satan is released from the bottomless pit for a short while.

As mentioned above, both mortal Gentiles and Jews will reside in the Kingdom. But the Jews as before will still be His Chosen. Jeremiah wrote about a "new covenant' which will take away their blindness toward knowing Jesus.

> *"Behold, the days are coming, says the Lord, when I will make a new covenant with the house of Israel and with the house of Judah- not according to the covenant that I made with their fathers in the day that I took them by the hand to lead them out of the land of Egypt, My covenant which they broke, though I was a husband to them, says the Lord. But this is the covenant that I will make with the house of*

Israel after those days, says the Lord: I will put My law in their minds, and write it on their hearts; and I will be their God and they shall be My people. No more shall every man teach his neighbor, and every man his brother, saying, 'Know the Lord,' for they all shall know Me, from the least of them to the greatest of them, says the Lord. For I will forgive their iniquity, and their sin I will remember no more."

Jeremiah 31:30-34

God gathered Jewish people from around the world to the Land that He promised them in the Abrahamic Covenant. They became a nation again in 1948, but they have never occupied all the Land that God has promised them *"from the river of Egypt to the great river, the River Euphrates." Genesis 15:18*. But at the beginning of Christ's Kingdom on earth, they will have all the Land that He promised them. The fulfillment comes thousands of years after the promise was initially made, but God is utterly faithful. Israel will be in full possession of the Land just as God said they would be.

The best thing about the Kingdom will be its King-Jesus. There has never been a perfect ruler on the earth, and this has caused much suffering throughout history. But the perfect King will rule His Kingdom in perfect truth and perfect justice. He will rule the world from Jerusalem eternally. When Gabriel appeared to the young virgin Mary, he informed her that her Son would reign on the throne of David forever.

> *"Then the angel said to her, 'Do not be afraid, Mary, for you have found favor with God. And behold, you will conceive in your womb and bring forth a Son and shall call His name Jesus. He will be great and will be called the Son of the Highest; and the Lord God will give Him the throne of His father David. And He will reign over the house of Jacob forever and of His Kingdom there will be no end.'"*

> *Luke 1:30-33*

What a wonderful promise that Gentiles along with the Jewish people can enjoy forever! He will rule in perfect effectiveness and in perfect peace.

> *"He shall judge between many peoples, and rebuke strong nations afar off; they shall beat their swords into plowshares, and their spears into pruning hooks; nation shall not lift up sword against nation neither shall they learn war anymore."*

> *Micah 4:3*

Scripture promises that Christ will gloriously reign from the Davidic throne. But Scripture also promises that the *saints* will reign with Christ. These will be people who are immortal and have a body like Christ's. It appears that there are two groups of "saints" that will reign with Jesus during the Millennium and beyond. The first are the ones that were Raptured-the ones in the Church Age that died in Christ and the Christians who will be alive at the Rapture. The second will be the saints that will be martyred for the sake of Christ during the Tribulation. These saints "missed" the Rapture but became Christians during the Tribulation and were killed because of it. I believe the first group of saints have this promise:

"Blessed and holy is he who has part in the first resurrection (Rapture). Over such the second death has no power, but they shall be priests of God and of Christ and shall reign with Him a thousand years."

Revelation 20:6

The second group that were martyred during the Tribulation will have this promise:

"And I saw thrones, and they sat on them and judgment was committed to them. Then I saw the souls of those who had been beheaded for their witness to Jesus and for the word of God, who had not worshiped the beast or his image, and had not received his mark on their foreheads or on their hands. And they lived and reigned with Christ for a thousand years."

Revelation 20:4

No one knows in what capacity we (immortals) will reign with Christ, but it may be related to the Judgement Seat of Christ when we will be judged for rewards. It may be commensurate with our faithfulness to Him during our earthly lives. It would be wonderful to hear the words from Christ: *"Well done, good and faithful servant. You were faithful over a few things; I will make you ruler over many things. Enter into the joy of your Lord"* Matthew 25:21

Scripture reveals that those who enter Christ's millennial Kingdom as mortals will enjoy some unique physical blessings. These are a few:

1. People will live in a blessed and enhanced environment.
2. Rain and food will be plentiful.
3. Animals will live in harmony with each other and with humans.
4. For mortals longevity will be greatly increased.
5. Physical infirmities and illnesses will be removed.
6. Prosperity will prevail, resulting in joy and gladness.

   (The End Times in Chronological Order, Ron Rhodes, Pages 198-199)

Perhaps the greatest blessing will be the privilege to worship the King of kings and Lord of lords with the whole world in His presence.

"For from the rising of the sun, even to its going down, my Name shall be great among the Gentiles; in every place incense shall be offered to My Name, and a pure offering; for My Name shall be great among the nations, says the Lord of hosts."

Malachi 1:11

PROPHECIES MADE	PROPHECIES FULFILLED
John 14:1-3 Christ is preparing a place for us in Heaven.	Yet to be fulfilled
Luke 1:30-33 The angel Gabriel promised Mary that the Eternal King would be born to her.	Luke 2:11 Jesus is born in Bethlehem.
Revelation 20:4,6 Christ shall have a thousand-year reign on the earth.	Yet to be fulfilled

QUESTIONS FOR DISCUSSION

How is a traditional Jewish wedding like the Rapture of the Church?

Can the environment make people right with God?

Will how we live in this life have anything to do with our lives in the Millennial Kingdom of Christ?

How will Christ rule in the Millennium?

CHAPTER 22: AFTER THE MILLENNIAL KINGDOM

As mentioned in the previous chapter, satan will be bound in the bottomless pit during the one-thousand-year reign of Christ. Revelation 20:3 indicates the reason for satan to be cast into the bottomless pit was so that "he would not be able to deceive the nations anymore until the thousand years were finished." After the Millennial Kingdom is finished, he will be released. Revelation 20:7-10 describes it this way:

> *"Now when the thousand years have expired, satan will be released from his prison and will go out to deceive the nations which are in the four corners of the earth. Gog and Magog, to gather them together to battle, whose number is as the sand of the sea. They went up on the breadth of the earth and surrounded the camp of the saints and the beloved city (Jerusalem). And fire came down from God out of heaven and devoured them. The devil who deceived them, was cast into the lake of fire and brimstone where the beast and false prophet are. And they will be tormented day and night forever and ever."*
>
> *Revelation 20:7-10*

Notice that all three persons of the satanic trinity are mentioned. The antichrist and false prophet will have been in the lake of fire burning for a thousand years already when satan joins them in the fires. Why did God let satan out? Remember, only believers will be invited into the Millennial Kingdom of Christ. These will be mortals that will reproduce in a perfect environment with a perfect ruler where sin will not be tolerated. But some of their children will hate Jesus. Over time a larger portion of the population will reject Christ in their hearts even though their actions will be good. When satan is released, a huge number follow him in rebellion against God. God quickly squelches the rebellion by sending down fire upon the rebels and they will be devoured. Perhaps the lesson to be learned from this is that a perfect environment cannot produce a perfect heart. Only by recognizing the need for forgiveness and submitting one's self to Jesus can the heart be changed.

So far, I have mentioned two judgements. The Judgement Seat of Christ or the Bema Seat of Christ and the Judgement of the Nations also called the Sheep and Goats Judgement. There is one more that no one would want to attend. It is called the Great White Throne Judgement. John wrote about it in this way:

> *"Then I saw a great white throne and Him (Christ) who sat on it, from whose face the earth and the heaven fled away. And there was found no place for them. And I saw the*

This is perhaps the saddest passage in the Bible. Even when Jesus hung on the cross, there was a glorious ending, but there is no happy ending for the wicked dead. These are the people who reject Christ's free gift of eternal life in Heaven. They knowingly trade the free gift of his grace for an eternal life in the lake of fire. There will be two types of books present at this judgement, the Book of Life and the Books of Works. There are two ways to gain eternal life in Heaven. One is to live a perfect life in this world. Only one Man did that. His name is Jesus. The other way is to accept His righteousness and have our sins forgiven through His sacrifice for us on the cross. Since this crowd of walking dead do not receive His grace because of their pride, their names will not be in the Book of Life. So, if they are to gain

Heaven, they would have to live a perfect life as Jesus did. And no one can. (All have sinned and come short of the glory of God!) The Books of Works will bear this out. Instead of allowing Jesus to stand the punishment that they deserve, they go their own way to destruction. There will be no excuses, and no one will have a defense. Jesus is the perfect judge. He is fair and they will sadly know it before they are thrown into the Lake of Fire forever and ever and ever and ever…….

There is only one question to ask ourselves as Christians. We know where some of our friends, family and neighbors will end up. Have we shared Jesus with them? The thought of their horrific future should be enough for us to overcome our fear of presenting the Gospel. Have you ever had an acquaintance die and you knew that they did not know Jesus? Did you feel guilty because you did not share the Gospel with them? I know I did.

CHAPTER 23: ETERNITY FUTURE

After the Millennial reign of Christ and satan is no more and all the judgements are complete, Heaven and earth will be renewed. Ever since sin entered the world through the works of the devil, there has been a curse on creation as we know it today. Since satan will reside in the lake of fire, he will no longer have any influence on the earth. But the earth will be full of evidence that he once was the ruler of this world. So, before the perfect "Eternity Future" begins, God needs to do some house cleaning. Peter said it the best when prophesied what this "house cleaning" will look like:

> *"The heavens and earth that now exist are stored up for fire, being kept until the day of judgment…The day of the Lord will come like a thief, and then the heavens will pass away with a roar, and the heavenly bodies will be burned up and dissolved, and the earth and the works that are done on it will be exposed. Since all these things are thus to be dissolved, what sort of people ought you to be in lives of holiness and godliness, waiting for the hastening the coming of the day of God, because of which the heavens will be set on fire and dissolved, and the heavenly bodies will melt as they burn! But according to his*

The Scriptures talk about three heavens. The first is our atmosphere. The second is the stellar universe and the third is the dwelling place of God. Only the first two have been touched by sin and satan, so they are the "heavens" that Peter talks about. There will be no need for the "Highest Heaven" to be renewed.

The new heavens and new earth will be the old heavens and earth that will be renovated by fire. The Greek word used for this renovation is *kainos* meaning "new in nature" or "new in quality." Since we will have new bodies that are free from a sin nature, so God's creation will also be new and free from all the sin stains that satan left on this earth. It will be absolutely perfect and glorious!

Our new bodies that we will receive at the Rapture will be designed to last forever. And we will live forever in the Heaven designed for us by God. The third heaven or New Jerusalem will be expanded to a 1500-mile cube that will rest on the renewed earth (Revelation 21:16). Evidently, we will be able to enjoy both places in total peace, total joy with no pain and no tears. We will experience the Glory of the Lord and be able to worship Him perfectly.

The beauty of Heaven will be beyond any human description. Chapters 21 and 22 is an attempt by John to describe its beauty. Remember the Tree of Life in the Garden of Eden? God had to cast out Adam and Eve from the garden and place a cherubim to guard it so that they could not come back to the tree of life. (Genesis 3:24) If they ate of the tree, they would live forever in their sin nature. God did not want that for them or anyone else in this world of sin. He reserved the tree of life for His renewed Heaven:

> *"And he showed me a pure river of water of life, clear as crystal, proceeding from the throne of God and of the Lamb. In the middle of its street, and on either side of the river, was the tree of life, which bore twelve fruits, each tree yielding fruit every month. The leaves of the tree were for the healing of the nations."*
>
> *Revelation 22:1-2*

We can then eat of that tree because our sin nature will be gone, and we will live forever!

One of the real joys we will experience in Heaven will be our reuniting with the believers we knew on earth. Seeing a favorite grandfather again will surely bring us great joy. Getting to meet believers that we did not know on earth will also be a blessing. And sitting down to talk to an ancestor that we never met will be thrilling. But the real thrill would be talking to Moses or Abraham or Jesus!

One of the greatest blessings that we will experience in Heaven will be to serve God. We will be in meaning service to Him. But it will not be like work on the earth for we will never be bored with our job, never get tired, never have to worry about being laid off or late for work. We will find our jobs exhilarating and we will always be motivated to do good things. Our main motivation will be the love we have for our Boss who we love and want to please, knowing that He loves us more than we could ever comprehend.

I am convinced that the little knowledge that we have about Heaven is but a drop in the ocean of what it will truly be like. Just knowing that God loves us and is waiting for us to see what awaits us should excite us beyond measure. What joy we experience at Christmas when we watch our little ones open the gifts that we purchased for them in love and see the joy and excitement on their faces. I cannot help but believe that God will experience the same joy when He watches us as we see our home in Heaven that Jesus Himself prepared for us!

All the joys of Heaven should overshadow the fear of death that we all experience at times. Anyone that has been diagnosed with cancer or other serious disease can understand the gripping fear and realization that we are mortal after all, and we will die sooner or later unless Jesus takes us up in the

Rapture. We should remember the promise of God, "I will never leave you or forsake you." Even in death He will be holding our hand.

I want to leave you with the comforting words of Jesus:

> *Peace I leave with you, My peace I give to you; not as the world gives do I give to you. Let not your heart be troubled, neither let it be afraid. You have heard Me say to you, 'I am going away and coming back to you." If you loved Me, you would rejoice because I said, 'I am going to the Father," for My Father is greater than I. And now I have told you before it comes, that when it does come to pass, you may believe.*
>
> *John 14:27-29*